PIONEERING WOMEN LAWYERS

FROM KATE STONEMAN TO THE PRESENT

PATRICIA E. SALKIN, EDITOR

ALBANY LAW SCHOOL

Commission on Women
in the Profession
American Bar Association
20th Anniversary ■ 1987-2007

Defending Liberty
Pursuing Justice

Cover design by ABA Publishing.

12 11 10 09 08   5 4 3 2 1

Cataloging-in-Publication data is on file with the Library of Congress.

Pioneering women lawyers: from kate stoneman to the present / Salkin, Patricia E., ed.

I am happy for the opportunity that I have had. Time, place and circumstances combined to help me accomplish my work. Up to my time there were many who tried to win and were unsuccessful. Later there were others who accomplished greater things. . . . My message is to younger women . . . they must take their opportunities as they come. Always there are opportunities to be had.

—Katherine Stoneman, 1925

Contents

Dedication

This book is dedicated to my children, Sydney and Jordan Gross, who I hope will be inspired in their generation to continue the vigilance and action that will lead to ensuring gender, ethnic, race and religious equity throughout their lifetime. It is also dedicated to the wonderful students, faculty, alumni and staff at Albany Law School who "walk the talk" every day to remove barriers for others and to advocate for fairness and equality for all people. Lastly, this book would not be a reality without the support and encouragement of my spouse and partner, Howard Gross, who has removed barriers of entry and glass ceilings for women and men and who has been an inspirational and tireless advocate for individuals with disabilities. Together, we can all continue to make a difference.

Acknowledgments

As the pages in this book will reveal, Kate Stoneman and the women she both inspired and "paved the way" for, are remarkable leaders who have each contributed to the inroads of women and minorities in the practice of law. Many people affiliated with Albany Law School, past and present, have brought vision and commitment, as well as dedicating countless hours to ensuring that the ideals and principles of Kate Stoneman remain at the forefront of our consciousness through education, scholarship and recognition. These people deserve special acknowledgment.

Our early pioneers in developing and implementing the annual Kate Stoneman Day—Mary Cole Dickerman, Carole Novick, Gail Bensen, Miriam "Mimi" Netter and Helen-Adams Keane—started and continue the proud tradition of highlighting issues and challenges confronting women in the law, as well as their contributions. Following the enthusiasm for Kate Stoneman Day, a group of faculty and alumnae set out to raise funds to endow a faculty chair at Albany Law School to honor Kate and to carry her beliefs into current times. Professor Mary Helen Moses co-chaired this effort with alumnae Donna Wardlaw and Dianne Phillips. Morris "Marty" Silverman provided the funding for a significant challenge grant that led to the establishment of the Chair. Support from former Albany Law School Dean Thomas Sponslor was also key to the success of the program. All of the people who contributed financial resources for this effort deserve our continuing appreciation.

In 2007, Albany Law School Professor Katheryn D. Katz became the first permanent Kate Stoneman chair-holder. Prior to that, the following visiting professors brought diversity in thought, teaching, and scholarship to Albany Law School as Kate Stoneman Visiting Professors in Law and Democracy: Marina Angel (2006), Qudsia Mirza (2004), Dianne Otto (2004), Justice Yvonne Mokgoro (2003), Penelope Andrews (2002), and Martha F. Davis (2000).

All of this work has been made possible by a committed and enthusiastic Kate Stoneman Committee. The committee has been chaired by incredible faculty members, including: Professors Patricia Youngblood Reyhan, Katheryn Katz, and Mary Lynch. Committee members over the years include Helen Adams-Keane, Jessie Aitcheson '95, Pamela Armstrong '86, Gail Bensen, Melissa Breger, Lenese Herbert, Karen Karl,

Katheryn D. Katz '70, Deborah Kelly '87, Kathe Klare, Mary Lynch, Joan Leary Matthews '83, Nancy Maurer, Connie Mayer, Dale Moore, Daniel Moriarty, Mary Helen Moses, Miriam Netter '72, Carole Novick, Nancy Ota, Alicia Ouellette '94, Dianne Phillips '88, Patricia Youngblood Reyhan, Patricia E. Salkin '88, Christina Sebastian, Laurie Shanks, Nicole Soucy, Donna E. Wardlaw '77, Tammy Weinman and Donna E. Young. Of course, these faculty, staff, and alumni are joined by the exceptional leaders of Albany Law School's Women's Law Caucus, who are active participants in all aspects of our Kate Stoneman programming.

In addition to the wonderful women who contributed their presentations to the chapters in this book, and to our President and Dean Thomas F. Guernsey for his continued support and involvement with the work of the Kate Stoneman Committee, special thanks to Michele Monforte of the Government Law Center, who helped me to organize this effort; David Singer, Albany Law School Director of Communications, for his editing assistance; and Professor Mary Lynch, for her enthusiastic support of this project. Our gratitude also to Stoneman Committee member Deborah Kelly '87 and the law firm of Hodgson Russ LLP for providing the transcription services for the speeches contained in this volume.

On a personal note, it has been both a privilege and a humbling experience to work with and to meet outstanding women who serve as inspirational role models for me and for countless other women in the legal profession. If Kate Stoneman was here today, she would most certainly be proud to know each of the people who have contributed in some way to opening up the legal profession and the development of the law to women and minorities. As you read the pages that follow, I am confident that you too will be warmed and inspired by the stories and the repeated reminder that our work is not yet done. Albany Law School has launched a Web site providing information about Kate Stoneman and those who have followed in her tradition. Please visit www.katestoneman.org.

Lastly, I am solely responsible for any errors in the editing of the speeches you are about to read. It is my hope that the minor editing of each set of remarks did not change the contributor's meaning or intent.

Professor Patricia E. Salkin
2008

Foreword

Albany Law School is very proud of its alumna, Kate Stoneman. The oldest law school in New York and the fifth oldest law school in the United States, Albany Law School has a rich tradition of providing educational opportunity to underrepresented groups.

As chronicled in this volume, Kate Stoneman, the first woman to be admitted to the New York State Bar, was a remarkable woman who serves as an inspiration more than 100 years later. At the time she graduated from law school in 1898, the extent of bias against women in legal education and the profession is hard to imagine. Only 1,010 lawyers in the United States were women.[1] New York, in spite of its generally progressive views, admitted Stoneman to the bar more than 30 years after the first woman was admitted to practice in Iowa.[2]

The depth of that gender bias is compounded by the fact that Albany Law School already had a sustained history of graduating (with the state bar admitting to practice) members of other underrepresented groups. Stoneman, for example, was preceded at Albany Law School by its first African-American, James Campbell Matthews, class of 1870. Matthews was a remarkable lawyer who two years later brought a lawsuit that desegregated Albany public schools.[3] Stoneman was also preceded by the law school's first Jewish student, its first Asian (Japanese) student, its first South American and its first Native American student.[4]

Stoneman's graduation in many ways was a pivotal point in Albany Law School's commitment to diversity. While Stoneman's admission was only the beginning of the inclusion of women at Albany Law School, it seemed to open a new wave of diversity. Albany Law School saw its first Chinese students in 1917 and 1918.[5] With Pedro G. Amador's admission to the class of 1902, the law school admitted more than two dozen Puerto Rican students over the next two decades.[6]

The period between the world wars was not one that legal education can look at with unbounded pride. It was not until World War II that women were again regularly admitted, albeit in small numbers. The first woman faculty member, while serving as the law school's librarian, began teaching legal bibliography, international law, and un-incorporated associations in 1950.[7] While only one woman graduated in 1945, this increased significantly to five in 1946. Five, though small in absolute numbers, was actually 18% of the class, and it should be kept in mind that Harvard did not admit any women until 1950. As late as 1963, there was only one woman in the Albany Law School graduating class, who happened to be the school's first female valedictorian.[8]

Again, as with most law schools, the progressive roots long dormant returned to life in the 1970s with the addition of two women faculty members, Sandra Stevenson (1974) and Katheryn Katz (1975). Professor Katz, the author of Chapter One of this book, has recently been appointed the Kate Stoneman Professor of Law at Albany Law School. The school's first African-American faculty member was hired in 1980[9] and its first African-American dean, John T. Baker, in 1991.[10]

This brief history is not offered to minimize the progress that the profession has made. It is offered to show the historical context in which Kate Stoneman was forced to operate. Indeed, it was not just within New York, but within the profession as a whole. Twenty years before Stoneman graduated from Albany Law School, just 20 miles north in Saratoga Springs, New York, the American Bar Association was founded on August 21, 1878.[11] The first woman was allowed to join 40 years later, in 1918.[12] It took another 77 years for a woman to become president of the ABA (1995-1996).[13]

Real progress in gender equity is a recent phenomenon. In 1950, 3% of the enrollment in the 120 ABA-approved law schools were women. In the next 20 years, that number had risen to only 8.6% of students in 146 ABA-approved law schools. Significant progress in gender diversity, therefore, is little more than 30 years old. By 1980, 34.2% of students in 171 ABA-approved law schools were women, and the number peaked in 2001 and 2002 at 49% in each of those years.[14]

Significant challenges for legal education and the profession remain to achieve true gender equity. Years of exclusion have had their effect. For example, while just short of half of all law school graduates are women (46.9% in 2006), in 2006 they formed only 29.4% of the profession (up from only 28.9% in 2000) and only 29.8% of American Bar Association membership (up only from 28.5% in 2000).[15] And, of course, women leave the profession in significantly larger numbers than men, and those remaining in the profession earn significantly less.[16]

In today's world, when half of Albany Law School students are women, it is easy to forget how remarkable Stoneman's achievement was. It is also easy to forget that she acts as a warning of the hard work ahead for true, and sustained, equality. We hope this book inspires everyone to engage in that hard work.

Thomas F. Guernsey
President and Dean
Albany Law School
2008

Notes

1. ROBERT STEVENS, LAW SCHOOL: LEGAL EDUCATION IN AMERICA FROM THE 1850S TO THE 1980S 83 (The University of North Carolina Press 1983).

2. *Id.* at 82.

3. ELIZABETH K. ALLEN & DIANA S. WHITE, ALBANY LAW SCHOOL: A TRADITION OF CHANGE 1851-2001 38 (Mount Ida Press 2000).

4. The students were, in order, Myer Nussbaum, class of 1877; Kozu Senzaburo, from Japan, class of 1877; Amara Cavalcanti, born in Rio de Janeiro, 1881 and later appointed Brazil's ambassador to the United States; and Alinton Telle, from Boggy Depot, Indian Territory, class of 1881, who compiled the first code of laws for Choctaw Nation. *Id.* at 63.

5. The students were Edward Jun Chu, 1917 and Hinting Wong, 1918. *Id.*

6. *Id.* at 70.

7. *Id.* at 110.

8. *Id.* at 109.

9. Professor Anthony Baldwin.

10. Henry Tseng, 1980, librarian; Alex Seita, 1983.

11. A Snapshot of Women in the Law in The Year 2000. *See* www.ABAnet.org (site visited October 2007).

12. Goal IX Report Card: An Annual Report on Women's Advancement into Leadership Positions in The American Bar Association, ABA Commission on Women in the Profession (February 2006).

13. *Id.*

14. *Supra*, note 11.

15. Goal IX Report Card.

16. In 2006, women attorneys earned 77.5% of that of their male counter-parts. Goal IX Report Card: A Snapshot of Women in the Law in the Year 2000 (ABAnet.org).

About the Editor

Professor Patricia E. Salkin is associate dean and director of the Government Law Center of Albany Law School, which she joined in 1990.

She teaches courses in land use law, housing law and policy, New York State administrative law, current legal issues in government, and government ethics. She is also on the adjunct faculty at the University at Albany in the department of Geography and Planning, where she teaches courses in planning law and planning ethics. Her prior New York government service includes the Office of Rural Affairs, Department of State, and State Senate. Dean Salkin is vice chair of the Municipal Law Section of the New York State Bar Association and a founding member and chair of the State Bar's Standing Committee on Attorneys in Public Service. She is also chair of the Special Task Force on Eminent Domain and a Special Task Force on Town & Village Justice Courts. Dean Salkin is active in the American Bar Association, and is a past chair and member of the Executive Committee for the State and Local Government Law Section. She is a member of the House of Delegates, a Fellow of the ABA, and was appointed to the Standing Committee on Membership. Dean Salkin is a reporter for the American Planning Association's Planning and Environmental Law publication, and she continues to serve as chair of the Association's Amicus Curiae Committee. She is the author of dozens of articles, chapters, and books on land use law, including the three-volume 4th edition of *New York Zoning Law & Practice* (1999) and the forthcoming five-volume *American Law of Zoning*. Dean Salkin has also served as a consultant on several occasions for the National Governor's Association, and recently served as a senior consultant to the National Academy for Public Administration on the intersection of environmental justice and land use planning and zoning. In 2004, New York State Court of Appeals Chief Judge Judith Kaye appointed her as vice chair of her Commission to Promote Public Confidence in the Judicial Elections. Dean Salkin's recent publications include *Land Use and Com-*

munity Development, 7th ed. (Thompson West) (with Nolon and Gitelman) (2008); *Current Trends and Practical Strategies in Land Use Law and Zoning*, ed., American Bar Association Publishing (2004); and *Land Use in a Nutshell* (Thompson West) (with Nolon) (2006).

Introduction

by Professor Mary A. Lynch

Professor Mary A. Lynch, clinical professor of law at Albany Law School and co-director of the Albany Law Clinic and Justice Center, is the co-chair of the Albany Law School Kate Stoneman Com-  *mittee. She received a B.A. from New York University and a J.D. cum laude from Harvard Law School. Prior to joining the Albany Law School faculty, Professor Lynch served as assistant district attorney in New York County from 1985 until 1989. Professor Lynch worked as an appellate and trial attorney in the district attorney's office. In 1997, while serving as director of the school's Domestic Violence Law Clinic, Professor Lynch and seven Albany Law School students won clemency for an incarcerated battered woman who killed her abuser. This marked the first time in New York that an incarcerated battered woman who killed her abuser was granted clemency. The second time that occurred was in 2000, when the New York state governor granted clemency to another client of Professor Lynch's clinic. Professor Lynch currently directs a Domestic Violence Prosecution Hybrid Clinic in which students are taught and trained to prosecute abusers. She has spoken nationally on issues concerning domestic violence and legal education and published articles concerning children with disabilities, constitutional jury issues, and teaching domestic violence prosecution. She is the recipient of awards from a local chapter of the National Organization of Women, the* Irish America *magazine, the Legal Aid Society of New York City for Outstanding Pro Bono Services, and the Hudson Mohawk Diversity Coalition.*

In 1866, three judges of the New York State Supreme Court held that neither "precedent" nor "necessity" required the admission of a woman, Katherine (Kate) Stoneman, to membership in the New York State Bar. Unwittingly, the court had unleashed the true and awesome power of "a woman scorned." As detailed in the background section of this book, politically and legally savvy, Kate Stoneman had anticipated the rejection and mobilized a coalition of suffrage workers, educators, and progressives to persuade the legislature to change the exclusionary stature. Within one day of the court's decision, Kate convinced the New York State Legislature and the governor to change state law to remove racial and gender prohibitions to admission. Following her legislative triumph, Kate Stoneman became the first woman admitted to practice before the courts of New York State.

Albany Law School has proudly embraced the legacy of Kate Stoneman, an 1898 graduate. Each year, we celebrate her triumph over exclusion, patriarchy, and overt discrimination by honoring exceptional women in the law, recalling current and former heroines, and appraising the current state of women and the law. That tradition is documented here in 12 inspiring speeches by a diverse set of pioneering and influential jurists, academics, bar association leaders, prosecutors, and government officials. Illuminating the pathway from 1866 to the present, the noted commentators describe human moments of exclusion and acceptance with poignant wit. They detail the unique challenges surrounding women and family, and communicate lessons of strategy, wisdom, and passion for justice. The Kate Stoneman tradition does not ignore the complex intersection of race, ethnicity and gender, and the speakers note these special complexities as they reflect on Kate's successful removal of both gender and racial bars to admission.

Exclusion and discrimination often sow the seeds of dissent, rebellion, and, ultimately, transformation. The stories of Kate Stoneman and her figurative "daughters" illustrate the lasting power of nonviolent rebellion against a system of exclusion and discrimination, demonstrating the progress women have made in transforming the legal landscape and claiming an equal place in and under the law.

Finally, the pioneering women lawyers whose thoughts and stories fill these pages foretell the challenges for future generations and inspire those of us, men and women, committed to ridding the legal profession of bias. As the Honorable Constance Baker Motley (Chapter 5) wisely reminds us, "The price of women's equality is eternal vigilance."

Professor Mary A. Lynch

Kate Stoneman:
A Pioneer for Equality

by Professor Katheryn D. Katz

Katheryn D. Katz, a professor of law at Albany Law School, was named Kate Stoneman Chair in Law and Democracy in 2007. For more than 30 years, Pro-*fessor Katz has been an award-winning teacher at Albany Law School. Among her curricular innovations have been courses on domestic violence—one of the first in the nation—and moral and legal issues in human reproduction. She has served on the New York State Governor's Commission on Domestic Violence; the Civil Rights Committee of the New York State Bar; the New York State Bar's Special Committee on Biotechnology and the Law; the Board of Directors of the Legal Aid Society of Northeastern New York; and the Committee on Research on Human Subjects at the Albany Medical Center. Professor Katz is the author of numerous articles on topics as diverse as the reproductive rights of minors, the First Amendment rights of students, majoritarian morality and parental rights, and elder abuse. Her scholarship in recent years has concentrated on assisted reproductive technologies and the law and includes works on surrogate motherhood, egg donation, the clonal child, and the legal status of the ex utero embryo. Professor Katz received an A.B. from the University of California, Berkeley, and a J.D. from Albany Law School. She was a Reginald Heber Smith Community Law Fellow and then went into private practice, founding one of the first all-female law firms in New York State.*

———————

In 1841 Kate Stoneman was born on the Stoneman farm in Busti in Chautauqua County, New York,[1] within sight of the grounds of the Chautauqua organization.[2] Kate had the misfortune to be born at a time when patriarchal principles governed women's role in society and defined relations between men and women. Women as well as persons of color were either barred from or not present in the major institutions of power: the government, the professions and the business and financial world.[3] At the time of Kate's birth, John Stuart Mill's seminal essay, The Subjection of Women, would not be published for another twenty-eight years. When one considers the time and place in which Kate was born, her accomplishments are all the more extraordinary. Fortunately, Kate was born in  upstate New York, which was to become the center of activity for the nascent feminist movement as well as the temperance movement. Although we honor her for her pioneering spirit in becoming the first female member of the New York bar, Kate was also an activist in three of the most significant reforms of our time: women's suffrage, the temperance movement, and the peace league movement.[4]

We know little of Kate's childhood beyond the fact that she was the fifth of eight children of George and Kathryn Rebecca Cheney Stoneman. We do know that Kate's parents were of English descent and were early settlers of Chenango County, New York.[5] Her mother's family were early Rhode Island settlers. Her father was a prominent lumber man and was for several years justice of the peace.[6] The town history reports that George Stoneman was "somewhat eccentric" and notes his successful construction of a "horseboat" using horses as the motive power to transport people around Lake Chautauqua.[7]

Two of Kate's brothers also achieved positions of distinction. In fact, until 1983 when the local chapter of the American Association of

University Women first recognized Kate as a member of its "Circle of Distinction,"[8] the name Stoneman was associated with George Jr., the oldest of Kate's brothers and sisters and twenty years her senior.[9] George, Jr. was a graduate of the United States Military Academy who became a career army officer, a Union general in the Civil War, and later served as Governor of California from 1883 to 1887.[10] George Stoneman Jr. was memorialized in a 1969 song, The Night They Drove Old Dixie Down, in a reference to one of Stoneman's Civil War raids: "Virgil Caine is the name, and I served on the Danville train, Till Stoneman's cavalry came and tore up the tracks again."[11]

Kate's brother John, the fourth child, was a graduate of Williams College who spent his summer vacations attending Albany Law School in Albany, New York. He was admitted to the New York bar in 1855; he then moved west and eventually became a judge of the Superior Court in Cedar Rapids, Iowa, after twice serving as a state senator.[12]

In a 1919 interview that chronicled her long fight for women's suffrage, Kate stated that she had been born into a "very liberal-minded" family that did not thwart her ambition to graduate from school.[13] Kate was admitted to the Albany State Normal School (now the State University of New York at Albany), a teachers' college in Albany, New York, in 1864 and the only state school in New York training teachers for the public schools.[14] Kate later recalled the journey from Busti to Albany in the middle of the Civil War as "very long and the traveling was quite perilous."[15] After graduating from the normal school in 1866, Kate spent a year teaching at the Glen Falls Seminary, and then began teaching at her alma mater.[16] She taught subjects that were typically taught by women in that era—geography, drawing and penmanship, rather than subjects requiring more intellectual rigor, as these were considered unsuitable for women. During her tenure at the normal school, Kate served as vice-principal for a time and had the distinction of being the first female president of the alumni/ae association.[17] Kate, however, was never promoted to professor.

KATE AND THE SUFFRAGE MOVEMENT

One of the animating themes of Kate's life was her effort to secure the vote for women. The cause of women's rights was in its infancy when Kate was a child. Before the Civil War a number of the women who supported the abolition of slavery also organized in support of their own political and civil rights.[18] The Seneca Falls Convention in 1848 gave birth to the campaign for universal suffrage that the organizers hoped would be the means of correcting other injustices. Susan B. Anthony declared that "the right which women needed above every other, the one indeed which would secure all the others, was the right of suffrage."[19] At the time of the Seneca Falls convention, the position of all females was marked by profound inequality and subordination. In addition to being unable to vote, women could not hold office, serve on juries or be admitted to institutions of higher education. Women were regarded as needing the guidance and control of husbands and fathers. Women had few opportunities to become self-supporting or to acquire property. Domestic service and farm work were the leading occupations for women.

The divinely ordained destiny of women may have been marriage and motherhood but a married female was particularly disadvantaged. A woman lost her legal identity upon marriage and came under her husband's "wing and protection" in the condition known as "coverture." Coverture placed restrictions on a wife that included being unable to sue or be sued in her own name, limited her ability to make contracts and losing all of her personal property and management of her real property to her husband.[20] The husband was head of the household with all that implied. He was the guardian of their children and had an absolute entitlement to their custody if the couple separated. Every privilege or pleasure that a wife enjoyed was either the husband's gift or depended entirely upon his will.[21]

Arguably, the adoption of the Fourteenth Amendment in 1868, which included a clause providing that no legal privileges or immunities could be denied a citizen, meant that women could no longer be denied the right to vote. The Amendment, however, failed to advance the cause of universal suffrage. In 1875 the Supreme Court rejected a challenge to the laws of Missouri which confined the franchise to men, stating that although women are citizens, the privileges and immunities clause did not confer suffrage upon anyone.[22]

Kate Stoneman became interested in women's suffrage after she began teaching and she continued her efforts until the franchise for women was secured. The cause of women's suffrage in New York achieved its first milestone in 1880 when the New York State Legislature passed a bill providing for women's participation in school elections.[23] This small victory inspired suffragettes to become more organized in their efforts to secure the franchise for women. Kate was a participant in the formation of the Women's Suffrage Society of Albany, a group which kept its independence from the nascent state organization.[24] The Albany society did send delegates to the state convention and subscribed to the organization's platform but kept its "organization intact and regulated [its] own policies, independent of theirs."[25] The suffrage society divided the legislators into small groups and its members lobbied individual legislators to support a suffrage bill.[26] Kate later said that the group "had the 'run' of the two houses" and its members could come and go as they pleased.[27]

Although the Speaker of the House, James Hustad, was an "ardent supporter" of women's suffrage, and although a suffrage bill was introduced in the legislature every year, it would be forty years before women received the equal franchise in New York. In 1918, New York gave women the right to vote. Kate served as poll watcher in Albany in the first election in which women voted. In 1920, the Nineteenth Amendment, giving women the right to vote in federal elections, was narrowly ratified and then signed into law by President Woodrow Wilson.[28] Unlike some of the early suffragettes, such as Susan B. Anthony, who died before women obtained the franchise, Kate was fortunate enough to live long enough to see her nearly lifelong quest for equality of voting rights become a reality.

KATE AND THE LEGAL PROFESSION: A TRAILBLAZER

While studying at the normal school Kate had obtained employment as a copyist for the state reporter of the New York Court of Appeals.[29] Since there were no typewriters at the time, various state offices used copyists who did work that would later be performed by stenographers.[30] Thanks to her excellent penmanship and her repeated readings of an old law book back in Busti while growing up, Kate "quickly became very proficient" at this work, for which she received ten cents a page.[31]

Kate's interest in the law also sparked her having been named as the executrix of a great aunt's estate while she was teaching at the normal school. She was guided in settling the estate by an old friend of the Stoneman family who, upon seeing her interest in legal matters, put his extensive law library at her disposal.[32] Kate began to read law in her spare time, during the summer, over the weekend and at night,[33] an undertaking which seems to have played a role in her decision to take the New York state bar examination. There was not one female lawyer in New York at the time Kate applied for admission to the bar in 1886, and there were very few in the rest of the country.[34] As Kate herself later remarked, the only occupations then open to women were "housekeeping, sewing, cooking, tailoring, domestic nursing, teaching in 'dame' schools and shop work."[35] The only other woman to have taken the New York bar had failed.[36]

Kate passed both the written and oral part in 1886 but was summarily denied admission to the bar solely because she was a women.[37] The three judges of the New York State Supreme Court, the court that held the power to regulate and admit attorneys to practice at the bar stated: "No precedent, No English precedent, No necessity."[38] Moreover, the New York Code of Civil Procedure required that an applicant for admission to practice be male.[39] Undeterred, Kate and her suffragist supporters began lobbying efforts to change the law.[40] Within a day she had found almost unanimous support in both houses of the legislature for an amendment stating that neither race nor sex could be an impediment to bar admission.[41] That same day Kate visited Governor David B. Hill, and Secretary of State Homer A. Nelson, who signed the bill. Shortly thereafter Kate took the signed bill to the Supreme Court and was duly admitted to practice by the same three judges who had earlier denied her application.[42] Thus Kate became the first female member of the bar in New York and one of the few women admitted to practice law in the United States.

Kate was wise to have sought legislative reform of the rules governing bar admission. Women in other states who had challenged in the courts the laws that blocked their admission to practice had not been successful.[43] The Supreme Court of the United States was equally unsympathetic to the cause of female bar applicants. Myna Bradwell, who had successfully passed the Illinois bar but been denied admission to practice because of her sex, petitioned the Supreme Court on the ground that the Fourteenth Amendment's privileges and immunities clause "open[ed] to every citizen of the United States, male or female, black or white, married or single, the honorable professions as well as the servile employments of life; and that no citizen can be excluded from any one of them."[44] Although the Court affirmed the denial of Myra's application on the ground that the federal government has no power to control and regulate the practice of law in the states, it is Justice Bradley's concurring opinion on the rights of women that has lived on (in infamy), particularly his statement that "civil law, as well as nature herself, has always recognized a wide difference in the respective spheres and destinies of man and woman."[45] Justice Bradley also opined: "The paramount destiny and mission of women are to fulfill the noble and benign offices of wife and mother. This is the law of the Creator."[46]

Upon her admission to the New York bar, Kate Stoneman received letters and telegrams of congratulations from all over the country.[47] Governor Hill, in a speech to the State Bar Association in 1887, welcomed "the fair sex in this new field of honor" and stated his hope that "the influence of women, usually so potent for good, shall be conducive toward arraying the whole profession more thoroughly on the right side... and the sphere of all women may well be more generally extended."[48] Kate's admission to the bar, however, was not unanimously praised. An article in the Daily Register, the predecessor to the New York Law Journal, compared the yearly changes in women's fashions to the practice of law by women. "It mockingly suggested that every year all legal documents would be changed to meet the latest fashions."[49] The *Albany Law Journal* congratulated Kate on her admission to the bar but "humbly" advised her "to have as few women clients as possible" since women clients are "troublesome."[50] It should be noted that while much has been made of the fact that Kate opened the door for women to practice law in New York, there is almost no mention of her equally important success in making certain that there was no racial barrier to admission to the bar.

After her admission to the bar, Kate decided that she needed further legal education and applied to Albany Law School. There had been other New York women before Kate who had wanted to study and practice law but who had to leave the state to do so.[51] The record shows that when three other women sought admission to Columbia Law School, they were summarily rejected. George Templeton Strong, the dean at the time, noted in his diary that three "infatuated women" had applied.[52] He went on to declare: "No woman shall degrade herself by practicing law in New York especially if I can save her."[53] In fact, three of the first women to practice law in the United States, Belva Lockwood, Lemma Barkaloo and Lavinia Goodell, were native New Yorkers who had to leave the state in order to realize their professional ambitions. After being rejected by Harvard and Columbia, Lemma Barkaloo moved to Missouri and became the first female law student in the United States when she enrolled at Washington University in 1869.[54] Belva Lockwood was the first woman to practice in the federal courts[55] and Lavinia Goodell was the first woman to practice law in Wisconsin.[56]

Even though she had an established legal practice, Kate Stoneman desired further legal education.[57] Accordingly, Kate applied to Albany Law School in 1896 and was accepted as a special student. At that time, many of the faculty at the school had legal practices or served as judges.[58] In an ironic twist, one of the professors was Judge Judson S. Landon, the judge who had ruled against Kate's admission to the bar in 1886. The 1897-98 school catalogue contained an announcement that Kate was a student and a statement that "sex is not a bar for admission to the school."[59] Kate continued to teach part time while taking classes. Kate received her L.L.B. in 1898, becoming the first female graduate of Albany Law School.[60]

Kate practiced law in Albany for many years in an office at 136 State Street. From 1889 through 1922, Kate was listed as a lawyer with an office in her residence at 134 South Swan Street in Albany.[61] Unfortunately, there are no records of her legal work and therefore we do not know how active her legal practice actually was.[62] Kate's "primary reason for her concentrated efforts to obtain admission to the bar was for the precedent it established and the new sphere of life which she opened to women."[63] Kate did not cease her work on women's suffrage and in the temperance and peace movements when she became a lawyer. She had been particularly pleased with the efforts to form a league of nations which she believed would bring about world peace.[64]

KATE AND THE TEMPERANCE MOVEMENT

Again, we do not have much in the way of historical records concerning Kate's role in the temperance movement. In the twenty-first century, it is easy to forget how important the cause of temperance was to women's rights. Between the end of the Civil War and the beginning of the twentieth century, the Women's Christian Temperance Union was the greatest force for enlarging the sphere of women.[65] The suffrage movement sought to enlarge the role of women in the political and social sphere; the temperance movement sought to strengthen the role of women in the domestic sphere by protecting the home from the harmful effects of excessive drinking.[66] Despite these differing notions of the proper role of women, the two movements attracted many women who were active in the cause of both suffrage and temperance. One of the most noted was Ada Kepley, the first women to graduate from law school in the United States, and an activist in the cause of women's suffrage and an organizer in the Women's Christian Temperance Union.[67] In fact, the "[t]emperance women were the earliest and largest single constituency to support the ballot for women[.]"[68]

There are popular images of members of the temperance movement as grim-faced "battle-axes" determined to spoil the fun of those who did not share their anti-hedonic views. It is true that many organizers, particularly the members of the Women's Christian Temperance Union, saw the drinking of spirits as degrading and immoral. It is also true that anti-Catholic and anti-immigrant sentiment drove the efforts of some temperance supporters.[69] Supporters of the temperance movement, however, were not uniformly or solely motivated by religious or moral beliefs or prejudice against more recently arrived immigrants. For many feminists temperance was important because excessive drinking led to abuse of wives and children, poverty and disease. Kate herself stated that she was a "believer in the 'logic' of prohibition, rather than the letter of it."[70] She continued: "It is not for myself that I want prohibition, nor for the men and women of temperate habits, but rather for the sons of women who have striven all their lives to keep their boys from the evil influences which surround the public house where liquor is sold. Therein lies the danger, I believe."[71] Although the repeal of prohibition was seen as a repudiation of the temperance movement, the movement accomplished goals other than prohibition that endure to this day, notably health education in the schools, including instruction about alcohol and the importance of exercise for women.[72]

KATE'S REFECTIONS ON HER LIFE AND TIMES

Toward the end of her life Kate remarked upon the revolutionary changes that had taken place during her lifetime: "I cannot quite realize that this is the same world then and now. Everything seems to have changed so very materially. . . . It is as though the minds of the universe had been taken out to air, and had imbibed some new germs which have universally taken hold. But I enjoy it with the rest of mankind, and glory in the fact that while I cannot take an active part in things now, I am able to appreciate what the changes are, and can still respond to them."[73]

Kate's last interview, published shortly before she died in 1925 at the age of 84, illustrates her modesty when she stated that "[t]ime, place and circumstances combined to help me accomplish my work."[74] What marvelous work it was. Kate is buried in Albany Rural Cemetery in Menands, New York. Rest in peace, brave pioneer, dear sister.

Notes

1. Christine Sebourn, Women's Legal History Biography Project, *Kate Stoneman* 2, *available at* http://womenslegalhistory.stanford.edu/papers05/StonemanK-Sebourn05.pdf.

2. Geraldine Muray, *Miss Stoneman, Pioneer Lawyer: First Woman in Profession Recalls Long Fight for Suffrage*, ALBANY KNICKERBOCKER PR., Feb. 19, 1919.

3. MONA HARRINGTON, WOMEN LAWYERS 3-6 (Alfred A. Knopf Publ'g 1993).

4. B. Dolores Thompson, *State's First Woman Attorney Was Born on Lakewood Farm*, March 12, 1983.

5. *Id.*

6. *See* Town of Busti, The Stoneman Family, http://www.townofbusti.com/stoneman.html.

7. HISTORY OF CHAUTAUQUA COUNTY, NEW YORK, AND ITS PEOPLE (John P. Downs & Fenwick Y. Hedley eds.) (Am. Historical Soc'y 1921), excerpt *available at* http:www.rays-place.com/history/ny/chau-busti.htm.

8. *See* B. Dolores Thompson, *The Circle of Distinction Welcomes Catherine Harris*, POST-JOURNAL (Jamestown, N.Y.), Mar. 10, 1984, *available at* http://www.prendergastlibrary.org/jamestown/catherinedickesharris.html.

9. *See* Town of Busti, The Stoneman Family, http://www.townofbusti.com/stoneman.html.

10. The California State Military Museum, George Stoneman, Jr.: Civil War General and California Governor, http://www.militarymuseum.org/Stoneman.html.

11. The Band, *The Night They Drove Old Dixie Down*, *on* THE BAND (remastered recording, Capitol 2000).

12. *Hon. John T. Stoneman*, *in* THE UNITED STATES BIOGRAPHICAL DICTIONARY AND PORTRAIT GALLERY OF EMINENT AND SELF-MADE MEN, Iowa volume (Am. Bio. Publ'g Co. 1878), *available at* http://www.rootsweb.com/~iabiog/iastbios/bd1878/bd1878-s.htm#JOHNTSTONEMAN.

13. Muray, *supra* note 2.

14. Geoffrey Williams & Carole Novick, *A Woman Who Wouldn't Take No for an Answer*, ALBANY L. SCH. MAG., Union Univ., Spring 1992.

15. *Id.*

16. *Id.*

17. Sebourn, *supra* note 1, at 3-4.

18. *See* The Association of the Bar of the City of New York, Women and the Law, http://www.nycbar.org/Library/FeaturedExhibitions2.htm.

19. *Id.*

20. NORMA BASCH, IN THE EYES OF THE LAW 17 (Cornell Univ. Press 1982).

21. JOHN STUART MILL, THE SUBJECTION OF WOMEN (Alan Ryan ed., Penguin Classics 2007) (1869). Text of John Stuart Mill's famous essay is available online at http://www.constitution.org/jsm/women.htm.

22. Miner v. Happersett, 88 U.S. 162 (1875).

23. Muray, *supra* note 2.

24. *Id.*

25. *Id.*

26. *Id.*

27. Sebourn, *supra* note 1, at 45.

28. *See* Sam Roberts, *1920: Women get the right to vote: the 19th Amendment was ratified 85 years ago, after decades of campaigning by the women's suffrage movement,* N.Y. TIMES Upfront, Sept. 5, 2005.

29. Sebourn, *supra* note 1, at 2.

30. *Miss Kate Stoneman, Lawyer, One of Pioneer Suffragists,* ALBANY KNICKERBOCKER PR., Nov. 19, 1916.

31. *Id.*

32. *Id.*

33. Muray, *supra* note 2.

34. Sebourn, *supra* note 1, at 39.

35. Williams & Novick, *supra* note 12.

36. *Id.*

37. *Id.*

38. *Id.*

39. Howard A. Levine, *The Regulation of Foreign-Educated Lawyers in New York: The Past, Present and Future of New York's Role in the Regulation of the International Practice of Law,* 47 N.Y. L. SCH. L. REV. 631, n.6 (2003).

40. Sebourn, *supra* note 1, at 46-50.

41. *See* 1886 N.Y. LAWS, ch. 425.

42. Williams & Novick, *supra* note 12; *In re* Stoneman, 40 HUN 638 (1886).

43. See, *e.g., In re* Goodell, 39 Wis. 232 (1875). Goodell's admission to bar was denied, the court stating that for a woman to forsake her "sacred" duties as a wife and mother was tantamount to "treason." A determined Goodell spearheaded a successful movement to have Wisconsin legislation enacted that prohibited denial of bar admission solely on the basis of sex. KAREN BERGER MORELLO, THE INVISIBLE BAR 26 (Random House 1986). Although Goodell was then admitted to practice, she died at the early age of 41. Some newspapers in reporting her death lauded her achievements, but the *Chicago Journal* could not resist suggesting that perhaps Goodell's death meant that women were unable "to endure the hard usage and severe mental applications" that attend a professional legal career. *Id.* Mary Leonard was another early female bar candidate. In 1885 she unsuccessfully sued for admission to the Oregon bar after having passed the local bar exam. *Id.* at 28. Undeterred, Leonard then lobbied for the passage of a bill that would permit women to practice law on the same terms and conditions as men. After successful passage of the bill, Leonard again

applied for admission. Denied on the ground that she did not meet a one-year residency requirement, Leonard argued her own cause before the Oregon Supreme Court. Impressed by her moving argument, the court granted her application and she become the first woman admitted to practice in Oregon. *Id.* at 28-29. Matters were no easier in the federal courts. Belva Lockwood had to get a bill through Congress in order for women to be allowed to practice in the federal courts. *Id.* at 31-35. On the other hand, a rare court victory secured the admission of Bella Mansfield, who successfully challenged a restrictive reading of the applicable Iowa statute in the court, thus becoming the first female admitted to practice law in the United States. *Id.* at 11-13.

44. Bradwell v. Illinois, 83 U.S. 130 (1872).
45. *Id.*
46. *Id.*
47. *Miss Kate Stoneman, Lawyer, One of Pioneer Suffragists, supra* note 20.
48. Williams & Novick, *supra* note 12.
49. Sebourn, *supra* note 1, at 52.
50. *Id.*
51. Morello, *supra* note 41, at 76.
52. *Id.*
53. *Id.*
54. *Id.* at 44.
55. *Id.* at 31.
56. *Id.* at 22-27.
57. Williams & Novick, *supra* note 12.
58. *Id.*
59. *Id.*
60. *Id.*
61. *Id.*
62. *Id.*
63. Sebourn, *supra* note 1, at 53.
64. *See* Williams & Novick, *supra* note 12.
65. Janet Zollinger Gielle, Two Paths to Women's Equality: Temperance, Suffrage, and the Origins of Modern Feminism 63 (Twayne Publishers, 1995).
66. *See id.* at 2.
67. Morello, *supra* note 41, at 50.
68. Gielle, *supra* note 63, at 3.
69. *Id.* at 94.
70. Muray, *supra* note 2.
71. *Id.*
72. Gielle, *supra* note 63, at 111.
73. Muray, *supra* note 2.
74. Williams & Novick, *supra* note 12.

Hon. Judith S. Kaye
1994

2

Honorable Judith S. Kaye, Chief Judge of the State of New York, was appointed by Governor Mario M. Cuomo in 1993 and reappointed by Governor Eliot Spitzer in 2007. She is the first woman to occupy that post, and in 1983 was the first woman to serve on New York State's highest court, the Court of Appeals. Chief Judge Kaye's current posts also include service as chair of the Permanent Judicial Commission on Justice for Children; founding member and honorary chair, Judges and Law-

yers Breast Cancer Alert (JALBCA); member of the Board of Editors, New York State Bar Journal; and trustee, The William Nelson Cromwell Foundation. She has served as president of the Conference of Chief Justices, chair of the Board of Directors of the National Center for State Courts (2002-2003), and co-chair of the Commission on the American Jury of the American Bar Association (2004-2005). She is the author of numerous publications—particularly articles dealing with legal process, state

---

Note: These remarks appear in 57 ALBANY LAW REVIEW, 961 (1994) and are titled "How to Accomplish Success: The Example of Kate Stoneman."

constitutional law, women in law, professional ethics, and problem-solving courts—as well as the recipient of many awards and several honorary degrees. Chief Judge Kaye engaged in private practice in New York City until her appointment to the Court of Appeals. She received a B.A. from Barnard College (1958) and an LL.B. from New York University School of Law (cum laude, 1962).

Forty-three young men and one young woman were graduated from the Albany Law School on the 2d inst., receiving their diplomas from the hands of Rev. A.V.V. Raymond, D.D., LL.D., president of Union University, of which the Albany Law School is a part. It was the 47th commencement of the school, one of the oldest and most famous in the United States, and one which numbers among its graduates hundreds of men who have reached high eminence, from President William McKinley down the honorable line.[1]

So began the *Albany Law Journal*'s report of a historic commencement, which took place on June 2, 1898.

In conferring the degrees, Dr. Raymond announced that Miss Kate Stoneman, that "young woman" of the class of 1898—then 57 years old, a teacher at the Albany Normal School for 32 years, and already a lawyer for a dozen years—was the first woman of any department in Union University to receive a bachelor's degree.[2] As Miss Stoneman stepped forward, modestly, to receive her parchment, the class members applauded loudly.[3] Prizes were awarded to several of the graduates, including an American and English encyclopedia of law, the grand sum of $50 for the highest standing in department and general study, and (my favorite) six volumes of American Electrical Cases for distinction in corporations.[4] Some class members, including the president, were not in attendance, having enlisted in the volunteer armed services, another announcement that drew hearty applause. Perhaps the reason for much of the enthusiasm and good cheer that day was what the *Albany Law Journal* characterized as an "agreeable innovation" at commencement exercises: "the elimination from the program of the usual orations."[5] Having myself twice delivered the commencement speech at Albany Law School, I can well appreciate the sentiment.

But indeed there was one speech to the graduates—and apparently an excellent one at that, described as "exceedingly interesting and helpful" (though, I might add, no applause is noted)—by Judge William J. Curtis, titled "How to Accomplish Success."[6] Regrettably, I have accomplished no success in locating that speech,[7] leaving us all to speculate wildly on what might have been said to and what might have been heard by (not necessarily one and the same) 43 young men and one young woman that day.

How to accomplish success naturally begins with one's definition of it, and definitions of success abounded then, as they do today. One prize-winning definition went as follows: "He has achieved success who has lived well, laughed often, and loved much."[8] But this was after all a law school graduation, and it is unlikely that law graduates were treated to such a short, lighthearted message. I suspect what they heard went more like John Adams's somber counsel a century earlier:

> Bend your whole soul to the institutes of the law and the reports of cases that have been adjudged by the rules in the institutes; let no trifling diversion, or amusement, or company, decoy you from your book; that is, let no girl, no gun, no cards, no flutes, no violins, no dress, no tobacco, no laziness decoy you from your books. . . . Labor to get distinct ideas of law, right, wrong, justice, equity; search for them in your own mind, in Roman, Grecian, French, English treatises of natural, civil, common, statute law; aim at an exact knowledge of the nature, end and means of government; compare the different forms of it with each other, and each of them with their effects on public and private happiness.[9]

I have tried to imagine Kate Stoneman among the graduates, absorbing that sort of advice or fitting her life into the context of a time when the occupations open to women were "housekeeping, sewing, cooking, tailoring, domestic nursing, teaching in 'dame' schools, and shop work."[10] A graduating class of nurses at Johns Hopkins University heard a much more fitting definition of success for women of the day: "Tact is the saving virtue without which no woman can be a success."[11]

Would Kate Stoneman have agreed that tact is the preeminent ingredient of success? From a study of her life, I strongly doubt it. Born in Lakewood, New York, in 1841, Kate Stoneman was the fifth of eight children of hard-working farm parents—born teachers devoted to learning and books.[12] She was determined from an early age herself to become a teacher and, between 1864 and 1866—Civil War years—made what she described as a "very long" and "perilous" journey from her home in Jamestown to the Normal School in Albany, the only state school in New York training teachers for the public schools.[13] In 1866, she began a teaching career at the Normal School (with a brief break at Glens Falls Seminary) that continued over the next 40 years, until 1906.[14] Her subjects included penmanship, geography, drawing, and school law. In 1925, at the age of 84, she died.[15]

Those statistics fit Kate Stoneman quite comfortably into a mold of success for professional women of the day—essentially a separate, distinctly "lesser" sphere. At the Normal School where she chose to spend half of her life, no woman reached the rank of professor, and the women were paid about half that of their male counterparts.[16] But those statistics only begin to portray this pioneering, precedent-setting, path-breaking individual. They obviously did not fit Kate Stoneman's own vision of success for herself or other women.

Kate Stoneman's interest in law began in her youth with one "huge, musty looking law book, which she read again and again, partly because it interested her and partly because [books being scarce] she had little else to read."[17] As a college student, she had another brush with the law: she put her splendid penmanship to use, working as a copyist at 10 cents a page for Joel Tiffany, state reporter for the Court of Appeals.[18] I've riffled the pages of volumes 28 to 33 of the New York Reports many times wondering, was it something in these cases that kindled the spark? Was it our beautiful courthouse or our magnificent courtroom that inspired her to tackle a seemingly insurmountable barrier and sit for the bar examination?

It was actually service as executor of her great-aunt's estate that directly precipitated Kate Stoneman's serious study of law for two years in the offices of Albany attorney Worthington W. Frothingham—nights, summers, and weekends—while continuing as a teacher.[19] But in fact by 1885, when she took the unprecedented step of sitting for the bar examination, she had long nurtured a thirst for the equality of women, and a vision of the potential for reform through law.[20]

Kate Stoneman's career as a suffragist began soon after she started teaching. It became the center of her life,[21] resulting even in discipline at the Normal School for teaching suffrage to students. Efforts to persuade the New York legislature to amend the laws that so entrenched women's inequality were a natural focal point.[22] As she later noted, "I think it is called lobbying now, but in those days it was the simplest thing in the world to get inside the brass rail. We had the "run of the two houses and were allowed to come and go as we pleased."[23]

That proved to be useful experience when, having passed the bar examination, Stoneman was refused admission because the Code of Civil Procedure allowed only "male" citizens to practice law and "her sex was against her."[24] With the legislature then nearing the close of its session, Stoneman and friends, in one day, walked a bill through both houses, changing the law to declare that race and sex would constitute no cause for refusing any person admission to practice.[25] And then—again accompanied by a cadre of supporters, including representatives of the press—she personally called on the governor and the secretary of state for their signatures. As reported, she spoke "briefly and concisely, but eloquently, representing the little group of serious minded women who were working for a voice in the affairs of government. It was chiefly to extend the field of women's activity that Miss Stoneman was anxious to gain admission to the bar."[26]

The bill was signed into law, and three days later—on May 22, 1886—Kate Stoneman was admitted to the New York Bar.[27] "A new day had dawned for the women of New York state, and from all over the country and from all types of people, telegrams and letters of congratulation poured in to Miss Stoneman."[28]

For the next several decades, Kate Stoneman kept an office on State Street in Albany, New York, where she carried on her educational work, law practice, and advocacy of world peace, but above all her struggle for the vote and for equality. What a sweet pleasure it must have been for her to serve as a poll watcher when, in 1918, women at last got the vote! When the chance was at hand for her to open yet another path—access to education—it was again irresistible.[29] Though already a member of the bar, she showed considerable fortitude by enrolling in Albany Law School as a first-year law student, and she well earned her place on the second of June among the Class of 1898.

A class note in the January 1925 *Alumni Quarterly of New York State College for Teachers*—the year of Kate Stoneman's death—sums up her life:

> There is little of personal glory and satisfaction in Miss Stoneman's story.[30] Rather, she rejoices over the fact that through her efforts she was able to pave the way for other women. "I am happy for the opportunity that I have had. Time, place, and circumstances combined to help me accomplish my work. Up to my time there were many who tried to win and were unsuccessful. Later there were others who accomplished far greater things. The present day presents greater opportunity than ever before for a woman. They are succeeding and will go on in their accomplishments. My message is to younger women. They must take their opportunities as they come. Always there are opportunities to be had."[31]

THE LESSONS OF HISTORY

Grant Gilmore describes history as a "systematic distortion of the past, designed to tell us something meaningful about the present."[32] So what meaningful lessons do we learn from the example of Kate Stoneman?

First, we know from looking back on her life that the differences from those days to these are striking, and that we have much to celebrate. Most striking of all is that, in the Albany Law School Class of 1898, there was one woman among 43 men. In the Albany Law School Class of 1998, there will likely be more than 100 women, perhaps half the class, perhaps even more. This year women comprise 47 percent of Albany Law School's graduating class, as they have in law schools throughout the nation for the past several years. For decades, women law students have been in the solid double digits, inching their way toward 50 percent of the class and beyond. In 1898, Kate Stoneman was the only woman admitted to practice in the entire State of New York, one of a few in the nation. It is predicted that by the year 2000, one-third of the nation's lawyers will be women.[33]

Facial change like that is evident in all corners of the profession. Women—plural women—sit on the United States Supreme Court, the New York Court of Appeals, the Appellate Divisions, and throughout the judiciary. Women lawyers are found in the highest reaches of academia, private law firms, corporations, government—even the White House. With law school enrollments hovering close to 50 percent women and 50 percent men, we are assured for the foreseeable future that these happy facts will continue.

Beyond facial change, we can celebrate that growing numbers of women have unquestionably made a genuine difference. While entry into all of the professions was difficult, not surprisingly, the legal profession—the "epicenter" of societal change[34]—was most resistant.[35] The public image of the "fair sex," the delicate, nurturing, "true woman" in need of the protection of a husband or father, just didn't jibe with the public image of the lawyer—"bold, brilliant, aggressive, incisive, ruthless," and courts denying women admission to the Bar had no reluctance spelling that out: that was, after all, the law of nature.[36] George Templeton Strong summed it up well at Columbia University Law School, in the year 1925. In his words, "No woman shall degrade herself by practicing law in New York especially if I can save her."[37] And as hard as it was to open the doors to legal education and admission to the bar, changing societal images—both the image of submissive women and the image of ruthless lawyers—has been the most difficult of all. But there too the differences have been striking and the gains worth celebrating.

In so many respects the laws have changed, the ground rules have changed, and (most impervious of all) public attitudes have changed, as the lines defining and separating two unequal spheres have blurred. It is no accident that the earliest women lawyers were also suffragists; access to government is elemental. But beyond the vote, it is clear that there has been significant progress toward the inclusion of women in places and institutions of every sort, in large part attributable to lawyers and the law. We have seen this even in our own lifetimes, as we have moved far beyond the vote and the right to serve on juries, to statutes and constitutional doctrines banning discrimination, and to society's recognition of marital rape as a crime, battered woman syndrome as a defense, and sexual harassment as a wrong. Indeed, the ground rules have changed very significantly from Kate Stoneman's days.

But if the definition of "success" is not simply inclusion and access, but also equal access and equal participation in vital decision making, there are other lessons in a study of history, and that is how much remains the same, how much there is yet to be accomplished.

Even in this day of breathtaking scientific and technological progress, the historic separation and inequality of the two spheres continues. As Chief Judge of the State of New York, I had a poignant reminder of this phenomenon recently when I dropped in at a Park Avenue club in Manhattan to meet a friend, and was told that no women are allowed in the dining room.[38] Much as I resent such experiences, the reminder is a useful one for those who may believe that the battles were all fought and won for us by Kate Stoneman 100 years ago.

The reminders are not hard to find. Even in the legal profession, where women have for decades been entering and practicing in increasing numbers, we see no natural, comparable progression of those numbers of women into the positions of power and influence—it is still a banner-headline event every time. With women a steady 30 or more percent of the law school graduating classes, surely we should expect that by now there would be far greater numbers of women who have become judges, major law firm rainmakers and partners, corporate presidents and general counsels, tenured faculty members and law school deans.

And most troubling of all to me, in my own 32 years at the bar, is that I see very little genuine advance in the area of family and child care issues, which are determinative in the careers of many women. As far as most employers are concerned, these still remain personal problems to be resolved by the families involved, and as far as most families are concerned they still remain the woman's problem to be resolved by her alone. I can well recall the wife of one of my partners, back in my own law practice days, expressing sympathy on the departure of my long-time housekeeper because it meant I would have to leave the firm.

Of course, many women facing that critical choice, with far less support than I had, do leave. A recent poll by the *New York Law Journal* reported facts we all know: lawyers regularly working around the clock, including nights and weekends, with little time for family and friends.[39] The women lawyers, far more so than the men, told of work-related stress behavior at home, and the women, far more so than the men, expressed the wish that they could work fewer hours for less money.[40] But the law firm culture persists virtually unchanged from my own entry into that world more than three decades ago, and the pressure is enormous—in some ways perhaps even greater than it was a century ago, when simply being the first itself defined success.

In preparing for today, I read a fascinating essay on Clara Shortridge Foltz,[41] California's first woman lawyer (admitted to the bar in 1878), and wondered how she managed to travel through the state and nation, breaking barrier after barrier, while raising five children. Twenty-four pages into the article I found the answer—her mother took charge of the babies,[42] a privilege not many of us have. Too many women still are discouraged by the prospect and reality of a demanding profession and society that remain very slow to change.

I have participated in endless discussions of these issues, several with my own lawyer-daughter, who, by the way, does not have a mother available to take charge of her babies. If anything, the discussion has grown infinitely more complex as women themselves part company over the very meaning of equality: does equality proceed from the proposition that we speak in a "different voice,"[43] or is the first premise that there is no difference at all between male and female lawyers.[44] Not one of my discussions has ever reached a satisfactory conclusion, or indeed any conclusion at all.

I have no greater expectation today. Though we continue to debate many of the same questions, and in fact merely proliferate the open questions, I am far happier participating in the discussion as Chief Judge, here in the presence of my extraordinary colleagues on the Court of Appeals, Judges Carmen Ciparick and Vito Titone, in a room filled with articulate men and women (many of them lawyers and law students) dedicated to finding the answers. I am far happier than Kate Stoneman must have been facing barriers to the vote, to the bar, to law practice, and even to a law school education. That so many of us have grappled with these issues, alone and together; that so many of us, beating our own individual paths through the thicket, have apparently made it into a clearing (or at least into another thicket), seems to me to bode well for the success of other women struggling with the same life-defining questions.

I have read a great deal about Kate Stoneman—indeed everything I could find which, as with much of women's history, regrettably tells us very little of what the real person thought and felt.[45] I believe, however, that she did, by the time of her Albany Law School graduation, have a very well-formed view of how to accomplish success, beginning with a dream, a vision of what could be accomplished, and buttressing that vision with courage, tenacity, creativity, and—when the occasion required—even a bit of tact. I suspect she could have added immeasurably to Judge William J. Curtis's commencement day observations on the subject, because she surely did know how to accomplish success, leaving for all of us—in a day when simply being first no longer defines success—the opportunity to do more, much more, in the pursuit of equality.

Notes

1. The Albany Law School Commencement, 57 ALB. L.J. 380 (1898).
2. *Id.*
3. *Id.*
4. *Id.*
5. *Id.*
6. *Id.*
7. I have been unable even to locate Judge Curtis in the annals of the judiciary.
8. Bessie Anderson (Mrs. Arthur J.) Stanley's prize-winning definition in 1904 contest conducted by BROWN BOOK MAGAZINE, in JOHN BARTLETT, FAMILIAR QUOTATIONS 905 (13th ed. 1955).
9. R. Carter Pittman, *Admissions to and Disbarments from the Bar of Justice,* 17 GA. BAR J. 169-70 (1954) (quoting John Adams (1759)). Small wonder that his son—John Quincy Adams—had mastered French, Greek, and Latin by the time he was 10 years of age. In the same vein, an 1898 article discussing the reading necessary for lawyers placed above all else The Bible (an "inexhaustible storehouse" from which to touch the conscience of juries); Shakespeare (again for quotations "to clinch . . . arguments and sway . . . juries"); a study of world history; ancient and modern literature; philosophy and the sciences (to make the lawyer a more profound thinker and more skilled reasoner); new novels; newspapers and magazines; and—somewhere on the list—law books. Walter L. Miller, *What Should Lawyers Read?,* 55 ALB. L.J. 279 (1898).
10. Geoffrey Williams & Carole Novick, *A Woman Who Wouldn't Take No for an Answer,* ALBANY L. SCH. MAG., Union U., Spring 1992, at 16, 17 (quoting MISS STONEMAN PIONEER LAWYER, ALBANY KNICKERBOCKER PR., Feb. 9, 1919).
11. Sir William Osler, in JOHN BARTLETT, FAMILIAR QUOTATIONS 743 (13th ed. 1955).
12. Williams & Novick, *supra* note 10, at 17; *see* Mabel Jacques Eichel, *Miss Kate Stoneman, Lawyer, One of Our Pioneer Suffragists,* 7 WOMEN LAW. J. 35 (1918) (originally published in ALBANY KNICKERBOCKER PR., Nov. 1916) (Mrs. Eichel was at the time press chairman for the Third Campaign District, New York State Woman Suffrage Party).
13. Williams & Novick, *supra* note 10, at 17; Eichel, *supra* note 12, at 35.
14. Williams & Novick, *supra* note 10, at 17.

15. *See id.* at 19.
16. *Id.* at 17.
17. Eichel, *supra* note 12, at 35.
18. *Id.*
19. *Id.*; Williams & Novick, *supra* note 10, at 18.
20. The women's rights movement officially began in 1848 at Seneca Falls, New York, when about 300 people, responding to the call of Elizabeth Cady Stanton and Lucretia Mott, passed a Declaration of Sentiments. 3 HISTORY OF WOMAN SUFFRAGE 67-73 (Elizabeth Stanton et al. eds., 1881).
21. *See* Williams & Novick, *supra* note 10, at 17-18. The opinion of Attorney-General Hamilton Ward, in 1880, denying women the right to vote in school elections was a catalyst for the formation by Kate Stoneman and several other women of an organization "to give needed information to women who may desire to assert their right to vote, and to conduct the campaign on behalf of women." *The Ladies Open the Campaign*, ALB. EVENING J., May 20, 1880; *see also Suffrage to Women: The Attorney-General's Opinion of the Scope and Application of the New School Act*, ALB. EVENING J., May 18, 1880 (printing the opinion of the Attorney General); *The Woman's Mass Meeting To-Day*, ALB. EVENING J., May 19, 1880 (listing the resolutions adopted by the new women's organization).
22. New York women gained the right to vote on January 1, 1918, when the amended Article II, 1 of the New York State Constitution, conferring equal suffrage on women, took effect. Congress did not ratify the Nineteenth Amendment until 1920. *See also* NORMA BASCH, IN THE EYES OF THE LAW: WOMEN, MARRIAGE, AND PROPERTY IN NINETEENTH-CENTURY NEW YORK (Cornell University Press, 1982) (developing a feminist legal theory based on an analysis of historical developments in women's rights).
23. Williams & Novick, *supra* note 10, at 18.
24. Note by the Reporter, following *In re* Leonard, 53 AM. REP. 323, 325 (Or. 1885).
25. Act of May 19, 1886, ch. 425, 1886 N.Y. LAWS 668. After the statute was amended, Stoneman reapplied and her application was granted. *In re* Stoneman, 40 Hun. 638 (N.Y. 1886). As Governor Hill later stated: "Our profession, with becoming gallantry, will welcome the fair sex in this new field of honor and usefulness which has been opened to them. . . ." Eichel, *supra* note 12, at 35.
26. Eichel, *supra* note 12, at 35.
27. Williams & Novick, *supra* note 10, at 18.
28. See Eichel, *supra* note 12, at 35.
29. *Id.* Several New York women unable to secure a legal education in New York State left and studied law elsewhere. *See* KAREN BERGER MORELLO, THE INVISIBLE BAR: THE WOMAN LAWYER IN AMERICA, 1638 TO THE PRESENT 76 (1986); Karen L. Tokarz, *A Tribute to the Nation's First Women Law Students*, 68 WASH. U. L.Q. 89 (1990).

30. Contrast that remarkable statement with Eichel's assessment of Kate Stoneman's influence:

> Few women have done more for the cause of woman's rights than Miss Stoneman, who was not only an early, active suffragist, untiring in her efforts and devotion to the cause, but was the first woman admitted to the practice of law in the State of New York and who, in gaining admittance to the bar, opened to women a new and unhoped for field of activity.

Eichel, *supra* note 12, at 35; *cf.* Barbara Allen Babcock, *Clara Shortridge Foltz: "First Woman,"* 30 Ariz. L. Rev. 673, 674 (1988) ("Wherever she went . . . she was prominent.").

31. *Alumni Notes*, Alumni Q. N.Y. St. C. for Teachers, Jan. 1925, at 17, 18 (quoting an unnamed Albany newspaper).

32. Charles R. McManis, *The History of First Century American Legal Education: A Revisionist Perspective*, 59 Wash. U. L.Q. 597, 599 n.11 (1981) (citing Grant Gilmore, *Law, Anarchy and History*, U. Chi. L. Sch. Rec., Autumn 1966, at 2).

33. Toni Carabillo & Judith Meuli, The Feminization of Power: Women in the Law 1 (1990). One hundred years ago there were about 135 female lawyers and law students in the United States. There are now about 157,000 female lawyers (21% of the profession) and 54,000 female law students (43% of the total). Judith S. Kaye, *Women in Law: The Law Can Change People*, 66 N.Y.U. L. Rev. 1929, 1937 n.34 (1991) (citing ABA Commission on Women in the Profession, Fact Sheet (1991)).

34. Mona Harrington, Women Lawyers: Rewriting the Rules 7 (1993).

35. In 1910, there were 1,500 female lawyers and almost 9,000 female doctors. Babcock, *supra* note 30, at 716 n.221 (citing Barbara Harris, Beyond Her Sphere: Women and the Professions in American History 110 (1978)).

36. *See, e.g.,* Bradwell v. State, 83 U.S. (16 Wall.) 130, 141 (1872) (Bradley, J., concurring); *In re* Goodell, 39 Wis. 232, 245-46 (1875).

37. Morello, *supra* note 29, at 76 (quoting 4 The Diary of George Templeton Strong 256 (Allan Nevins & Milton H. Thomas eds., 1952)).

38. A bill first introduced 14 years ago to ban discrimination by many private clubs in New York State has been reintroduced in the state legislature this year. *See* Kevin Sack, *Measure to Bar Bias by Private Clubs Is Gaining in Albany*, N.Y. Times, Mar. 10, 1994, at B8; *see* N.Y.S. Club Ass'n v. City of New York, 505 N.E.2d 915 (N.Y. 1987), *aff'd*, 487 U.S. 1 (1988).

39. Edward A. Adams, *Legal Career Exacts Steep Personal Price*, N.Y. L.J., Feb. 7, 1994, at 1.

40. *Id.* at 2.

41. Babcock, *supra* note 30.

42. *Id.* at 696.

43. *See, e.g.,* CAROL GILLIGAN, IN A DIFFERENT VOICE (1982); Carrie Menkel-Meadow, *Excluded Voices: New Voices in the Legal Profession Making New Voices in the Law*, 42 U. MIAMI L. REV. 29 (1987).

44. *See, e.g.,* CYNTHIA HARRISON, ON ACCOUNT OF SEX: THE POLITICS OF WOMEN'S ISSUES, 1945-1968, at 3-23 (1988) (describing division over the Equal Rights Amendments); Sandra Day O'Connor, *Portia's Progress*, 66 N.Y.U. L. REV. 1546 (1991); *see also* Babcock, *supra* note 30, at 677 (describing two early national suffrage associations that operated separately because women of that time could not agree on methods and ideologies for pursuing the vote). It's not at all surprising that very basic divisions persist: we are not a monolith.

45. It continues to disappoint me that no law school (to my knowledge) has, as yet, undertaken to establish a definitive collection on women in the law. Research in the area remains spotty and difficult.

Hon. Jeanine F. Pirro
1995

3

Honorable Jeanine F. Pirro is the former district attorney of Westchester County. First elected in 1993, she served in the position for three terms. Ms. Pirro was the first woman district attorney in Westchester County, the first woman Westchester County court judge, the first woman to try a murder case in Westchester County, and the first woman in New York State to be named "outstanding prosecutor." In October 1997, as chair of the New York State Commission on Domestic Violence Fa-  *talities, she issued a comprehensive report providing detailed recommendations and resulting in the passage of legislation to enhance protections and provide safeguards to victims of domestic abuse. Ms. Pirro previously was an assistant district attorney in Westchester for several years, beginning her work in the Westchester District Attorney's office in 1975, just after graduating from Albany Law School. She headed the domestic violence unit, which was the first in New York State and one of only four in the United States at that time. Her tenure as Westchester district attorney was marked by a 28% decline in violent crime, attributable to her creation of a number of special units to prosecute specific types of crime. Ms. Pirro is the author of a book,* To Punish and Protect: A DA's Fight Against a System that Coddles Criminals, *in which she urges reforms of the legal system to allow for easier prosecution of criminals. Ms. Pirro has appeared on several television shows as a legal commentator.*

It was a very happy memory for me when I walked into Albany Law School this afternoon. The nicest memory is that I met my husband at Albany Law School. We're still together after 20 years and we have two children, dogs, a few fish and some birds. Our son, Alex, came into the bedroom a few months ago and he said to me, "Ma, I know what I'm going to be when I grow up." So I asked (thinking, probably a Power Ranger or a Ninja Turtle), "Okay Alex, what do you want to be when you grow up?" He said, "Mom, when I grow up, I want to be the D.A." He said, "But Ma, can boys be D.A.'s?" Isn't that a great story? It makes me realize just how full circle we've come and how things have changed. Our nine-year-old daughter, Christy, came home and she said, "Mom, now that I'm in fourth grade I can be an altar boy?" So, I thought about the fact that my son wants to do something that he thinks girls do and my daughter wants to do something that she thinks boys do, and I said to my husband, "Al, we have to spend a little more time at home."

It's wonderful to be back and to talk about how far we've come. It was not much more than 100 years ago that the United States Supreme Court upheld the constitutionality of a statute that prohibited women from practicing law. And therefore the words from our Declaration of Independence that "all are created equal and endowed with certain inalienable rights" yielded no life, liberty, or pursuit of happiness to those women when the doors to the legal profession were closed because of their sex. And it was not until 1920—75 years ago—that women gained the right to vote. Imagine telling your daughter that she couldn't vote because she was a female. Imagine a country where women were considered incompetent to testify as witnesses in our courts. I'll give you a little history on that one. The reason women were considered incompetent to testify in courts was because they did not have testicles upon which to square. And that's where the word "testimony" comes from. Since women couldn't swear or testify on their testicles, then they could not testify in court. That's true! Imagine a country where women couldn't own property, sign a contract, or keep their own earnings. Where wives were shot, stabbed, beaten, and brutalized with no criminal consequences to their abusers. Where children were raped and sodomized with legal license and where sexual harassment at the workplace was considered a fact of life and not a legal wrong. And where it was a crime to beat your wife only if you beat her after 10 p.m.

When I came to Albany Law School, one of the first things I learned in the law of contracts, a class taught by Professor Semerad, was that silence is not acceptance. Over the years, I have learned that there are many applications of this principal. Women in the evolution of their journey to have what the law of morality dictates is rightfully theirs, have witnessed this principal at work. Although silence has never been acceptance, silence has inadvertently reinforced inequality. Although it was never acceptance, the silence of victims of domestic violence and the silence of victims of rape who were afraid to come forward, led to a system which acquiesced in the victimization of women. The truth is that, even in this year—1995—equality within the criminal justice system remains a goal rather than a reality. And so, today, the real challenge is more difficult than the effort it took to educate the men who made the rules. It is to educate those of us who have already reached some degree of success to not be silenced by that success. Today the real danger is being silenced by tokenism or moderate success. With such complacency comes the silence and the continued distance in the quest for equality.

It is 1995, and yet we are living in a time when a state survey finds that sexual bias is pervasive in our courts. We are living in a time when less than 40 women sit in Congress, with 504 men. And we are living in a time when it was only five years ago that Medicare mandated that insurance cover mammograms, while EKGs covering what is considered primarily a male disease, were covered for decades. We are living in a time when women still earn only 67, 68, or 69 cents, depending upon the study that you look at, for every dollar that men earn. We are living in a time when female victims of assault are questioned about irrelevant sex practices. Where a deceased's diary receives almost as much attention as the fact of her murder itself. And when overly vigorous cross-examination of victims turns into harassment on the witness stand with the resultant message to others: maybe it's better to not come forward. The theory then, that silence is not acceptance, is too passive for 1995.

We are living in an era when silence is a flaw. But we have the power to change things simply by speaking out. When I was a little girl growing up in Elmira, people used to ask me what I wanted to be. I was part of the first generation of children to grow up with a television and I focused on one show for my hero, and that was "Perry Mason," because Perry Mason defended the underdog. And so I answered, "A lawyer." And the response was always the same, "But don't you want to be a mommy?" And so I grew up thinking that the two were mutually exclusive. I grew up thinking that I had to be one or the other. But those are the truths of yesterday that we change, all of us, every day, as we progress in the profession. And when I came to Albany Law School I learned that all of society was to be judged by the "reasonable man" standard. That in both the civil and the criminal law, the way to examine behavior and thinking was to use the only appropriate standard, that being the "reasonable man" standard. And if you did not conform to this standard, you lost. But those are the truths of yesterday.

As an eager assistant district attorney 20 years ago, I found that the truths that I learned here in Albany about equal justice and equal rights are ever so far removed from the reality of life for thousands of innocent, helpless victims of crime in our world today, many of them too young to even articulate the horrors that are inflicted upon them. I was told that child abuse was a social problem and not a criminal justice problem. I was told the crimes against children were better handled in civil courts where there is no punishment. That children can't testify because it's too frightening for them. After all, how could we be sure that they weren't lying? That women aren't strong enough to follow through with criminal charges. After all, they probably enjoyed the abuse. And that women who claim they were raped couldn't be believed or trusted unless there was an eyewitness who corroborated their story. That child pornography doesn't market in the United States, but only in European countries. But those were the truths of yesterday.

When I joined the district attorney's office in 1975, immediately upon graduating from Albany Law School, I was told the criminal justice system did not discriminate against women, although domestic violence was not considered a crime legally, morally, or politically. The reality was that physical violence occurs between members of the same family more often than it does between any other category of individual or any other setting, except for wars and riots. One is more likely to be killed by a member of his or her family, especially a spouse, than by any other category of individual. When we started this program, which was the first in the nation, I did some research on domestic violence because there was so little out there. I found out that in 2,500 B.C. if a woman was verbally abusive to her husband, her name would be engraved on a brick which would be used to knock out all of her teeth. In medieval Europe, all legal systems agreed that a man had both a legal and a moral right to beat his wife, so long as he beat her with a stick that was no thicker than his thumb, thus the "rule of thumb." For me, it was time to change the rules and time to take sides. In the words of Elie Weisel, "To do nothing helps the abuser, never the victim. Silence encourages the tormentor, never the tormented." Thus, we built the bridge with the Domestic Violence and Child Abuse Bureau, constructed of blueprints brought to us by mental health professionals, social service professionals, and law enforcement, as well as victim agencies. We challenge the truths of yesterday and demolish them in our effort to construct new truths for tomorrow. Still today, however, across this nation, crimes against women are not prosecuted or are prosecuted without conviction. Still today, there are too many children living in fear—not of the street mugger or the stranger rapist—but of a loved one in their own home. That place which should be a haven in a heartless world. Children go to sleep every night in their own beds to become victims of unspeakable torture and abuse.

We can no longer accept things the way they are or be satisfied with where we are. We can no longer stand by and say that nothing can be done about crime or simply that we live in a violent society or that victims are people who somehow put themselves in a bad place. We can no longer stand witness to our children being shot and stabbed and beaten and brutalized by a stranger, or by a family member. It is said that as women and as mothers we are sensitive to those issues that affect us as women. Sensitive to those issues which affect our children. But we are more than one-dimensional. We are concerned with the global issues that affect the quality of our lives as human beings. This includes hate crimes and bias crimes, environmental crimes, drunk driving, drug crimes—and all other violent crimes.

So, ladies and gentlemen, it is time to take sides. It is time to get involved. There are many challenges that we face as we move into the future. Kate Stoneman was a pioneer and a trailblazer. Her dedication and perseverance forged the way for all of us, for me, as for so many women lawyers. As the first woman elected to the Westchester County Court bench and the first woman district attorney of Westchester, I can appreciate how far our country has come since Ms. Stoneman became the first woman admitted to the bar in New York. I am honored to be here today. I am delighted to return to my alma mater. Kate Stoneman Day provides an opportunity for me to encourage students and alumni, as I was encouraged here at Albany Law School, to pursue their goals and to set a standard of expertise and ethical conduct that makes us proud members of this honorable profession and not afraid to deal with the tasks that lie ahead.

M. Catherine Richardson
1996

4

M. Catherine Richardson currently is retired from the law firm of Bond, Schoeneck & King. Ms. Richardson has assisted hospitals in mergers and consolidations and ad-*vised medical centers on corporate and medical staff bylaws, credentialing of medical staff and allied health professionals, investigations of Article 28 deficiencies, and contracts between health care providers and consumers. She has worked on the formation and certification of an HMO and regularly advises insurance companies and HMOs regarding New York State insurance law and public health law. Her honors and affiliations include the Justinian Honorary Law Society (National Honorary), Order of Coif, SUNY Oswego Chapter of Phi Kappa Phi, The Delta Kappa Gamma Society International (Honor Society for Women Educators), Kappa Delta Pi (National Education Honorary), and Lambda Sigma Tau (National Mathematics Honorary). She is on the Board of Governors and a Fellow of the American Bar Association, past president of the New York State Bar Association and the Onondaga County Bar Association, and a Fellow of the New York State Bar Foundation. Ms. Richardson is the recipient of a number of awards, including the 2000 Ruth*

G. Shapiro Memorial Award (NYSBA), the 1996 Syracuse University Law College Association Distinguished Service Award, the 1995 SUNY Oswego Outstanding Alumni Award, the 1995 Syracuse Law Review's Alumni Achievement Award, and the 1994 Spirit of American Women Award - Girls Inc. of Central New York. She is a member of the board of the Bertholon-Rowland Corp. and a member of the St. Camillus Health & Rehabilitation Center, among other associations. Ms. Richardson is a graduate of Syracuse University College of Law (J.D., magna cum laude, 1977), the University of Northern Colorado (M.A., 1969), and the State University of New York at Oswego (B.S., 1963).

CHOICES, CHALLENGES AND CHANGE: HOW CAN TODAY'S KATE STONEMANS OPEN DOORS TO OPPORTUNITY?

A musty old law book, a decision to make the long and "perilous" journey from Jamestown to Albany to study teaching, service as an executrix, an appetite for taking on a challenge, and an unwavering determination to blaze trails to access new opportunities for women. These were the keys to Kate Stoneman's achievement in unlocking the door to admission of women as lawyers in New York State.[1] Hers was a life of zealous advocacy with an exclamation point.

An inspiring teacher, a successful lobbyist, a fervent suffragist, and, at age 45, a new lawyer, Kate Stoneman gave us a lesson in applying our skills, not only to the case at hand, but also to promote improvement in the law, the legal system, and equal opportunity.

If she could join us today—a century and decade later—how would she assess our efforts to carry on her work? What advice would she impart to us in handling both the enormous pressures and the subtleties experienced as we approach the 21st century?

I, too, have been perusing some musty old books and some newly minted studies in considering Kate Stoneman's outstanding adventure, the reaction in her day, and her impact over the years.

The brittle pages recording the proceedings of the New York State Bar Association's 1887 annual meeting[2] contain the observations by Governor and State Bar Association President David B. Hill about what he termed "an important innovation" enacted by statute. "Under the laws of 1886, women could no longer be denied admission on the basis of gender," Governor Hill stated. "At least one woman has already been admitted under the provisions of this act, and there are now female law students in various parts of the state."

His brief remarks on this subject did not identify the new lawyer as that dynamo, Kate Stoneman; nor did he note that, when her application for admission was denied because the law referred to male citizens, she promptly lobbied for this remedial legislation and, upon its passage, within two days personally carried the bill to the governor for his signature.[3]

In his address to the just 10-year old state bar association, the governor commented on the potential of the new statute:

> If the presence of ladies as associate workers in our profession shall tend to develop among us that true politeness and dignified courtesy which should always characterize the demeanor of the members of so honorable a calling towards each other, then the experiment will not have been made in vain. If the influence of women, usually so potent for good, shall be conducive towards arraying the whole profession more thoroughly on the right side of every public question, the sphere of women in all occupations may well be more generally extended.[4]

I am sure I am on solid ground in assuming there is general agreement that this effort has, indeed, not been made in vain and that the benefits and progress gained through the participation of women have taken us safely beyond the experimental stage.

I also believe that, as envisioned, the increased presence of women at the bar and on the bench has helped expand opportunities for women in other pursuits, as well as bringing a more intimate understanding and experience in addressing the legal issues affecting women. But as each door is opened, the issues become more complex; progress no longer occurs in leaps and bounds, but instead slowly inches forward.

The number of women passing through the door of admission that Kate Stoneman opened has grown in the profession from a handful at the end of the 19th century to almost one quarter of the bar and almost half of the law school classes today.[5] With this growth came strivings to attain and go beyond partnership and management levels, choices in practice areas, considerations in balancing family and professional responsibilities, and, following in Kate Stoneman's footsteps, the growth of second-career lawyers.

I shifted from being a high school math teacher to a practitioner in business, education, and health law. I made the trip from central New York to Albany today, but in less time and without the dusty, jarring, perilous ride experienced by our predecessor, Kate. With the fast pace and advancements, however, our journeys today and yours tomorrow are risky in a different way.

One hundred years after Kate Stoneman received her license, the Task Force on Women in the Courts, formed by then New York State Chief Judge Lawrence H. Cooke, issued in 1986 a study with a starkly worded conclusion: ". . . gender bias against women litigants, attorneys and court employees is a pervasive problem with grave consequences. Women are often denied equal justice, equal treatment, and equal opportunity."[6] The report called for actions to remedy problems relating to matrimonial, support, custody, and domestic violence matters, and treatment of women in the profession. The state bar association presented a companion report the following year, proposing initiatives that bar associations could take to pursue change in legislation and procedure, and expansion of opportunities.[7]

Both reports served to focus attention on gender-related concerns. Both cited the value of coordinated efforts of the courts, law schools, bar associations, government, and the community. A decade later, we still need to address the areas of concern with this same cooperative approach.

During this past decade, we can measure progress in the implementation of a number of the proposals. The Task Force and State Bar Committee recommended amendments to the Lawyer's Code of Professional Responsibility specifically proscribing discrimination and addressing the inappropriateness of biased conduct. The Ethical Consideration and proposed Disciplinary Rule were designed to give notice of "the seriousness of the impropriety and the consequences to the administration of justice."[8] In 1990, the Appellate Divisions enacted a Disciplinary Rule substantially as recommended.[9]

A call for similar changes in the Code of Judicial Conduct was proposed in both reports and renewed by the state bar in 1993. It is heartening to learn that revisions to the code promulgated by the court system last month include prohibitions of a judge's biased conduct and calls on the judge to direct attorneys and others in the courtroom to refrain from this behavior.[10]

Yet directives are only partial remedies. The greater challenge is in chipping away at the obstacles and misperceptions that cause glass ceilings and the less-than-hospitable environments that women continue to report encountering each day in their legal careers.

It seems like only yesterday, but in 1990, I participated in a forum focusing on career development issues for women entering law firms, seeking partnership, and further advancement.[11] We discussed means of dealing with the frustrations and assumptions that a female attorney can face with respect to her confidence and commitment; developing a style that suits her, while handling the mixed messages as to whether this approach is perceived as too aggressive or too timid; and balancing her professional and personal responsibilities and considering what impact those choices may have on her career path. The panel concurred that there appeared to be progress on the horizon, although slow in coming and requiring perseverance. But we also saw a growing incidence of women with great talent and potential who were leaving firms before being considered for partnership. And we recognized that perspectives and needs differ among the generations of women in the profession and among those entering practice. One panelist recalled that the five women in her law school class fought so hard to get in and be taken seriously that it would never have occurred to them to change direction.

And now, six years later. "Discrimination continues to permeate the structures, practices and attitudes of the legal profession. Creating awareness of discrimination has not eliminated bias from the workplace," the American Bar Association Commission on Women in the Profession concluded in a study that showed women behind in compensation and positions of authority.[12] A study of New York law firms found equality in the numbers and pay of men and women at the entrance level, but slippage on the higher rungs of the career ladder. There were slight increases in the proportion of women partners, but "minuscule" numbers of management. "There are many problems both men and women face today in achieving career success, but men do not face the stereotyping and negative expectations that women do," observed author Cynthia Fuchs Epstein in her examination of the glass ceiling.[13]

Even more distressing are reports that animosity at the law student level continues to persist. There was hope that obstacles might dissipate or at least diminish with the emergence of a younger generation—more aware, more politically correct, more understanding.

In a report revealing both bright spots and troubling conditions, a second ABA commission report cited changes that have made the climate in legal education more conducive to the full participation of women students and faculty. Yet the commission also found that "many women still experience debilitating instances of gender bias and discrimination in law schools," with some observers contending that overt hostility is more common than when the number of female students was small.[14]

This state of affairs shows how far we have come and how much more needs to be accomplished. Studies and informal conversations demonstrate that we are still grappling with the problems raised in that 1990 program. But the road of progress has become steeper and the challenges for women are compounded as a result of the current climate of belt-tightening, downsizing, fierce competition, a focus on the bottom line, and, in some cases, a struggle for survival.

We must double and triple our efforts to ensure that Kate Stoneman's cause is not relegated to a back burner. She would have hoped that, by this time, gender would not still be a factor that could derail advancement. We are at a critical crossroads. Beyond the potency of individual advocacy, what can be done? Bar associations, through their members, have a wealth of practical experience and insight that can help prepare students and new attorneys. Last spring, I participated in a program presented by the state bar's Committee on Women in the Law to provide tips to students and new attorneys on rainmaking techniques and the impact of gender in litigation styles. Attorneys were eager to serve as panelists; there was no shortage of questions from 200-plus attendees. Attend these programs—if they aren't available locally, ask the bar association for some help in planning one.

The Committee on Women in the Law also conducted a forum in February in New York City to give women law students information on what is involved in pursuing different career paths, what they might encounter, and ways of handling situations. The panelists' advice was solid: be prepared, know the hurdles, be yourself, learn and do well at every juncture, follow your aspirations, and don't shy away from charting your own course. Above all, they paraphrased Kate Stoneman, who told women to "take their opportunities as they come" for "always there are opportunities to be had."[15]

The state bar plans to do more for law students, and encourages bar organizations, alumni groups, and others to do likewise. However, it is not enough to ensure that students and new admittees know what positives and negatives they may encounter and how to maximize their potential.

Firms, government offices, and businesses need to assess their operating procedures and objectives and make modifications, in light of contemporary concerns and conditions. Law firms cannot afford to lose talented women lawyers and can only gain from having a diversity of perspectives and background. As Fuchs Epstein contended in her study, "Probably many firm managers do not look beyond everyday pressures, nor do they recognize the patterns of their own behavior and those like them. They may also be unaware of the consequences of their behavior, especially when they make decisions that they regard as even-handed."[16]

There is a need for more programming, resources, and discussions on workplace issues. As one step to aid attorneys and firms, our association has provided sample policies on childbirth and parenting leave, alternative work schedules, and sexual harassment, to aid and encourage attorneys and firms in the review and, where needed, revision of written policies.[17] We must emphasize, however, that the availability of family-friendly policies needs to be coupled with provision of a level playing field of opportunities for advancement.

Law office economics and management programs and resources offer another avenue of education. Effective and contemporary workplace procedures and means of enhancing inclusiveness and diversity should be a regular component of law office skills training—for firm management in particular as well as members of the bar in general. The tailoring of some forums and materials for management will underscore the importance of firms keeping attuned with and considering these issues on an ongoing basis. The development of mentoring programs through bar organizations and firms also should be encouraged.

Beyond policies, education and organized mentoring, there is another ingredient integral to opening doors of opportunity. Ask a woman who has achieved partnership or other level of advancement to identify the important stepping stones to her progress; invariably, she will tell you about the informal initiatives of more senior women and men who extended helping hands and offered counsel. It is incumbent upon us, as individuals, to reach out and assist "up and coming" attorneys. It is incumbent upon us, in firm management meetings and other venues, to raise issues and consciousness about the gender impact of conduct, contemplated changes in procedures, or lack of change.

As reports and anecdotal accounts clearly relate, difficulties in opening doors and cracking glass ceilings are not exclusive to the legal profession, but are the concerns of professions, businesses, and workplaces of many shapes and sizes. Although women and persons of color represent two-thirds of the population and 57 percent of the workforce in the nation, women comprise only five percent of senior managers in *Fortune* 2000 industrial and service companies.[18] Obviously, the need for greater change to foster inclusiveness can be translated into bottom-line terms of maximizing opportunity to reach and be relevant to the marketplace and attract and retain the best and brightest. While the increased focus on the bottom line has been damaging to the image and effective functioning of the legal profession in many ways, this is an area in which we should join with the business community in reshaping the structures and procedures and, most challenging, to dispel misperceptions to ensure level playing fields at every opportunity.

As we strive to pursue Kate Stoneman's mission, we can take inspiration from another adamant advocate for women's rights, Abigail Adams, who wrote to her husband John in the year of our country's independence, "In the new Code of Laws which I suppose it will be necessary for you to make I desire you would Remember the Ladies, and be more generous and favorable to them than your ancestors."[19] Today, we need to ensure that the pursuit of women's advancement in the profession is not viewed as yesterday's news. This seems the perfect time to renew our commitment to take every opportunity to counsel our colleagues on the importance of "Remembering the Ladies" in building a profession that is indeed inclusive; reflective of different experiences and perspectives; and effective in addressing the needs of clients and society, today and tomorrow.

As members of the bench and bar, we work incessantly to reform the law to meet contemporary conditions. We must demand no less of ourselves in reshaping our profession. As we go forward, let all of us here make a commitment to Kate—to work zealously—to extend a hand to those who follow—to speak out as a voice for equality.

Notes

1. Mrs. Mabel Jacques Eichel, *Miss Kate Stoneman, Lawyer, One of Our Pioneer Suffragists*, ALBANY KNICKERBOCKER PR., November 1916.
2. N.Y.S. BAR ASSOCIATION REPORTS—PROCEEDINGS OF THE TENTH ANNUAL MEETING OF THE ASSOCIATION (Jan. 18-19, 1887), Vol. X, p.40.
3. *Eichel, supra* note 1.
4. N.Y.S. BAR ASSOCIATION REPORTS, *supra* note 2.
5. As of 1995, women constituted 23% of the lawyers and 44% of the law students in the nation. ABA Commission on Women in the Profession.
6. Task Force Report (March 31, 1986), page i.
7. Report of the Special Committee on Women in the Courts (June 1987).
8. *Id.* at 271 n.6.
9. Disciplinary Rule 1-102(A):

   A lawyer shall not . . . (6) Unlawfully discriminate in the practice of law, including in hiring, promoting or otherwise determining conditions of employment on the basis of age, race, creed, color, national origin, sex, disability, marital status, or sexual orientation. Where there is available a tribunal of competent jurisdiction, other than a Departmental Disciplinary Committee, a complaint of professional misconduct based on unlawful discrimination shall be brought before such tribunal in the first instance. A certified copy of a determination by such a tribunal, which has become final and enforceable, and as to which the right to judicial or appellate review has been exhausted, finding that the lawyer then engaged in an unlawful discriminatory practice shall constitute prima facie evidence of professional misconduct in a disciplinary proceeding.

10. Ethical Consideration 1-7:

    A lawyer should avoid bias and condescension toward, and treat with dignity and respect, all parties, witnesses, lawyers, court employees, and other persons involved in the legal process.

    Daniel Wise, *Bias Amendments Added to Judges' Conduct Code*, N.Y. JOURNAL, Feb. 6, 1996, at 1, quoting the new Rule:

    A judge in the performance of judicial duties shall not, by words or conduct, manifest bias or prejudice, including but not limited to bias or prejudice based upon age race, creed, color, sex, sexual orientation, religion, national origin, disability, marital status or socioeconomic status, and shall require staff court officials and others subject to the judge's direction and control to refrain from such words or conduct.

11. "Women in Law Firms: From Law School to Partnership and Beyond," presented by N.Y.S. Bar Ass'n Committee on Women in the Law (Jan. 17, 1990).

12. Unfinished Business: Overcoming the Sisyphus Factor (December 1995), p.3.

13. Robert Saute, Bonnie Oglensky and Martha Gever. *Glass Ceilings and Open Doors: Women's Advancement in the Legal Profession*, Fordham L. Rev. (November 1995), at 439.

14. Elusive Equality: The Experiences of Women in Legal Education (January 1996), p.2.

15. *Alumni Notes*, ALUMNI Q. (January 1925) at 18.

16. *Id.*, at 447 n.14.

17. COMMITTEE ON WOMEN IN LAW, CHILDBIRTH AND PARENTING LEAVE: A REPORT AND MODEL POLICY (October 1990); SEXUAL HARASSMENT: A REPORT AND MODEL POLICY FOR LAW FIRMS (October 1992); REPORT AND SAMPLE POLICY ON ALTERNATIVE WORK ARRANGEMENTS (June 1995).

18. A SOLID INVESTMENT: MAKING FULL USE OF THE NATIONAL'S HUMAN CAPITAL (Recommendations of the Federal Glass Ceiling Comm'n (November 1995)), pp.9-10.

19. March 31, 1776, *quoted in* ADAMS FAMILY CORRESPONDENCE 1:370 (L.H. Bullerfeld ed., 1963).

Hon. Constance Baker Motley 1997 **5**

Honorable Constance Baker Motley, at the time of her death in 2005, was a district judge for the U.S. District Court, Southern District of New York.

Following her judicial appointment in 1966, Judge Motley was made chief judge of the U.S. District Court for the Southern District of New York in 1982 and senior judge in 1986. As a prominent civil rights attorney, Judge Motley won nine of the ten cases she argued before the U.S. Supreme Court, including the 1962 case in which James Meredith won admission to the University of Mississippi. In 1966 she became the first black woman to become a federal judge. Born to West Indian immigrants, she was an outstanding student, but her parents could not afford to send her to college (her father was a chef at an exclusive Yale University fraternity). After graduating from high school, she took a position with the National Youth Administration. Philanthropist Clarence Blakelee, impressed by Motley's intelligence and oration, offered to finance her education. She enrolled at Fisk University and transferred to New York University, where she earned a B.A. in economics in 1943. She went on to Columbia Law School, where she met Thurgood Marshall, who hired her as a law clerk

*law clerk at the New York branch of the NAACP Legal Defense and
Educational Fund. She remained with the fund after graduating in
1946. Judge Motley wrote briefs for the* Brown v. *Board of Education
(1954) case. In 1964 she was elected to the New York State Senate, the
first black woman to do so, and in 1965 she became the first woman
president of a Manhattan borough.*

I was in Albany, New York, some time ago, in 1964 and 1965 as a
member of the New York State Senate. At that time, I was still a member of the staff of the NAACP Legal Defense and Educational Fund
and still arguing cases before the United States Supreme Court. I had a
case that came up before the Supreme Court. I think it was *Wayne v.
Alabama*, the one case I lost before the Supreme Court. It was later
reversed on another case from Kentucky. But, anyway, I had a case
coming up in the Supreme Court and I had been there on eight occasions before that, if not nine. And I was sure that having been elected
to the senate, and with wide publicity in the *New York Times* and here
and there, that Chief Justice Warren would probably ask me whether I
would like to be addressed as Senator Motley or Mrs. Motley as he
had been calling me. So, I tried to prepare myself for his question, but
when I got up to argue that case, Chief Justice Warren simply said,
"Senator Motley," and so he wanted to indicate to me, I guess, that he
kept up with the news, too.

When I finished Columbia Law School in June 1946, if a poll had
been taken of those least likely to succeed in the profession, I would
have headed the list. World War II had ended in August 1945. The
men who had been drafted or dropped out of school and volunteered
to serve in the armed forces had returned in September 1945 or February 1946. The women and blacks who had been admitted during the
war were now overwhelmingly outnumbered at the law schools. In
other words, things seemed to be back to normal. I had been admitted
in February 1944, after graduating with honors from NYU/Washing-
ton Square College in October 1943. Because the war was on, all of
the universities had school year 'round and I finished college in two
and a half years as a result. I started college a year and a half after I
graduated from high school. In February 1944, I was admitted with
about 16 others in the middle of the year, half of whom were women.

There were probably about 20 women all told in the three classes. I can think of at least five of those women who were on *The Law Review*. Bella Abzug, a former member of Congress, was on *The Law Review* and graduated in June 1945. It is my recollection that she did not get a job with a Wall Street firm like some of the men who were on *The Law Review*. The first man in our class was a Jewish man. He didn't get one either. I recall going for an interview at a midtown firm in Manhattan that was seeking a law graduate. Some of the other women had already gone down, you know how it is, word gets around, where you might get a job when you graduate, and they had been down for an interview. So I called, and they made an appointment for me to be interviewed. When I entered the reception area and was standing at the receptionist's desk, I saw a door behind her open. A man peeked out and quickly closed the door. I don't remember what the receptionist said, she probably said something like, "The job has been filled." The pollsters, however, would have been correct, and I would have agreed with them, and that is because none of us had a crystal ball. None of us could have foreseen that post-war America would be convulsed by two revolutions—one which would carry blacks and the other which would carry women into the mainstream of American life. And that by 1997, there would be two women on the Supreme Court. About 100 women would be sitting on the federal benches around the country. And the same number with respect to blacks. And that the legal profession would be approximately one-third women and most of the law schools would have an enrollment of 50 percent women.

I had the good fortune of securing a position as a law clerk in the NAACP law offices, then headed by Thurgood Marshall, who became the first black to sit on the United States Supreme Court in 1968. He previously had served as the first black solicitor general. President John Kennedy had appointed Thurgood Marshall to the Second Circuit in December 1961. And then President Johnson appointed him to be solicitor general. Because of the opposition of Senator Eastland, who was chairman of the Judiciary Committee, Kennedy had been unable to get Marshall confirmed by the full senate to a seat on the Second Circuit at the end of 1961. And so Marshall initially got an interim appointment. After Marshall's appointment to solicitor general, President Johnson had sought to appoint me to the Court of Appeals for the Second Circuit. As the *New York Times* explained at the time, there was so much opposition to my appointment that Johnson had to withdraw my name. He then submitted to the senate my name for appointment to the district court. My name had previously been submitted by Senator Robert Kennedy in February 1965 while I was in the state senate, having been elected in February 1964's special election.

In February 1965, the New York State Senate had not yet organized itself due to its failure to select a senate majority leader. This was because in the Johnson landslide election in November 1964, the Democrats had gained control of the senate for the first time in 30 years. Also, in that landslide election, Robert Kennedy had been elected the new senator from New York, splitting the Democratic party statewide. Robert Wagner, who was the mayor of New York City at the time, of course, had desired to follow in his father's footsteps and had desired to become the second Wagner to serve in the United States Senate. Robert Kennedy, having been elected from New York, became a major figure in the Democratic party in the state and he sought to get his man appointed majority leader, while Wagner, who had been in effect the leader of the Democratic party, sought to get his man appointed. I finally voted with the Wagner forces to elect the Democratic Party Minority Leader, Joseph Zarefsky of Manhattan, who had been minority leader for at least 20 years, to the position of majority leader. We all understood that when the next election came around and there was no landslide by the Democrats, the Republicans would undoubtedly regain control of the state senate. So we were talking about a Democratic majority leader for two years. Since the Democrats could not agree on a candidate after six weeks, Governor Rockefeller made a deal with the Wagner forces to supply Republican votes to get Zarefsky elected. It was then that Robert Kennedy, who had submitted my name to Johnson for the district court, kind of abandoned me for that nomination.

There had been no opposition to my going to the district court, and so, as indicated, Johnson took up that nomination and sent my name to the senate for confirmation. Eastland was still chairman of the Judiciary Committee. At that time, Eastland held up all blacks nominated to the federal bench whether they had been actively involved in civil rights litigation or not. Since I had been prominently involved in civil rights litigation, especially in Eastland's home state of Mississippi, in a suit against the University of Mississippi, which had refused admission to James Meredith because of his race, Eastland saw to it that my name did not come out of his committee. Finally, rumor had it, that Johnson refused to send any more names to the Judiciary Committee until Eastland let my name out. This of course brought pressure on Eastland from other senators who were interested in getting their candidates onto the federal bench. Johnson had nominated me at the end of January 1966. I didn't get confirmed until August 1966 and was sworn in on September 9 of that year.

In February 1966, when the fight among the Democrats was continuing in the senate, there occurred a vacancy in the office of the president of the Borough of Manhattan. The eighth city councilman in Manhattan voted shortly thereafter to have me fill that vacancy. I thus became the first woman to be a borough president. I remember when the woman who was borough president of Queens (I can't recall her name, that's one of my problems today) was elected, the *Daily News* had a big headline: "First Woman Borough President Elected." When I was elected borough president, my picture was on the front page of the *Daily News* under the headline, "First Woman Elected Borough President." So, you see how well the *Daily News* does its research, right? And as I told you before I had been elected to the senate a year before in February 1964, at which time I was the only woman in the senate, though a few other women had previously been elected to the senate. In November 1965, I had to run for the office of borough president for a full four-year term, which I did, with the endorsement of the Democratic, Republican, and Liberal parties. And I served in that post until I was finally sworn in in September 1966 to the federal bench.

The stories I have about my encounters with racism and sexism since I have been on the bench are legion. But, of course, I have time for only a few. The first one I want to tell you about involved the practice of the judges of our court to meet for dinner two or three times a year at the Century Club in Manhattan. The Century Club, as you undoubtedly know, is a club founded in the last century by literary men—writers, artists, and so forth—which did not admit women to membership. The judges in our court were able to go there to dinner after the regular judges' meeting in the courthouse because we had one or two judges who were wealthy enough to pay the membership fee. They belonged so they could get a room for a dinner party. Some of the judges went there because the gourmet dinners then were exquisite. The menu included everything from hors d'oeuvres and drinks to cigars at the end. And I used to take a cigar for my husband because he smoked cigars then. The dinners were held in a room on the second floor of the club. That particular room had a long table to which leaves could be added so that it could seat up to 30 people. At that time, our full compliment was 24 judges on our court. Since I was the first woman on our court, the club's policy of not permitting women to attend functions above the first floor therefore presented real problems for this dinner. Just after I was sworn in, in September 1966, by then Chief Judge Sylvester Ryan, we had a new chief judge the next day, Sidney Sugarman. And after Sidney Sugarman got to know me pretty well a couple of years later, he told me how they managed to get me in. He told me that the judges engaged in a little deception. The dinner committee of judges told the powers that be at the Century Club that I was the secretary and that I would be attending the dinner meeting to take the minutes. And that's how I got above the first floor. This was a deception because the business meeting of the judges was held in the courthouse at 4 o'clock each month and then, as I said, about three times a year, we adjourned and went to the Century Club where we had this great dinner, which then cost only $25—today it's like $100. So, we don't go there anymore! You know we judges don't make that kind of money.

Now the next incident I want to tell you about is the one involving my invitation to attend the Patent Lawyers Annual Dinner. The patent lawyers had a custom of inviting the federal judges to their dinner every year, and they certainly expected the newly appointed judges to show up. At that time there were very few women in New York who were members of the patent bar. When the patent lawyers met for their dinner, the women patent lawyers were required to sit in the balcony. This dinner was usually at the Waldorf Astoria, and the women couldn't sit on the main floor with the men. When I was confirmed as a federal judge, there were only four other women in the country who were federal judges. One was Florence Allen, an NYU graduate who had been appointed by Roosevelt in 1936 to the Court of Appeals for the Sixth Circuit. Another was Sarah Hughes in Dallas, Texas, who swore in President Johnson when Kennedy was assassinated in Dallas in

1963. Another was Burnita Matthews, a judge on the district court for the District of Columbia. The fourth was Mary Donlin of the Customs Court in Manhattan. The patent bar, therefore, never having had a female judge before, made elaborate plans for me to be escorted to the dinner and escorted through the receiving line. The powers in charge of the annual dinner first wanted to send a young patent lawyer to my apartment to pick me up and drive me to the Waldorf. I told the person who called that it would not be necessary for the young patent lawyer to come to my west side apartment since they had invited my husband and he had a car and we had been to the Waldorf on many occasions while I was borough president. In fact, my husband had to get two tuxedos we went to so many dinners at various hotels in New York, particularly the Waldorf. We then agreed that the young man would meet me in the foyer of the grand ballroom and escort me through the receiving line. When my husband and I arrived in the foyer, we rehearsed with the young man how we would proceed. This young man was kind of nervous because in the past when there was a new federal judge who was a man, there was no problem—his wife would follow behind. So we rehearsed and the young man said, "Now look, I suggest that I go first and Judge Motley you come behind me, and I will announce that you have arrived to the president, who will be the first man on the receiving line and then I'll introduce your husband." The speaker for the evening on that occasion was William Henry Hastie, a black judge, who at that time was the Chief Judge of the Third Circuit in Philadelphia. He apparently had not arrived for the dinner that evening yet, so we proceeded and when the young man reached the president, before this young patent lawyer could say a word, the president jumped in and said to me, "Good evening, Mrs. Hastie." The young man was trembling next to me. I looked up at him, he had beads of perspiration on his forehead. He was so flustered he couldn't speak. I therefore said to the president, "I'm Judge Motley and this is my husband, Mr. Motley." One woman was assigned to sit with me and my husband on the main floor (at least they let me sit on the main floor). All the other women had to sit in the balcony.

When I was borough president I was invited to attend the annual dinner of our local newspaper reporters, the Inner Circle, because they invited all the city officials. And at that dinner they would roast the mayor. Mrs. Happy Rockefeller and I were made to sit in the balcony in 1965.

Another incident I want to tell you about was the lunch I attended and that was given by the Lawyers Club, which met in an office building on lower Broadway. The Lawyers Club, which of course consisted only of men, had a dining room where they had lunches and so forth, and they had a custom of inviting new federal judges to lunch whenever one was appointed. Marvin Frankel had been appointed the year before and so they were just getting around to inviting him when I got on, and so they invited me to attend the same luncheon. When I got on the elevator of this building on lower Broadway, I said to the elevator operator, "Twenty, please." (That is where the Lawyers Club met and where they told me to come.) The operator responded, "No women on twenty." I told him that I had been invited to the Lawyers Club. Well, of course that didn't mean anything to him. The elevator passed the 20th floor and I was asked to step out of the elevator on the 21st floor. Well, there's nobody on the 21st floor. In fact, it was dark and no lights and so forth. But there was a staircase to the floor below, the 20th, and I could hear people talking of course and see lights and so forth. And soon somebody came up from the 20th floor to escort me down. They didn't say anything.

The other story I want to tell you about is a criminal case I had some time in the '70s. The man to be tried had been charged with attempting to assassinate the President. We were in the process of selecting a jury to hear that case. We had seated several jurors in the jury box. I had excused one or two prospective jurors for cause when the name of a middle-aged woman was drawn, who then took her seat in the jury box. She spoke with a slight accent, so I gathered she was European. I said to the new prospective juror, as we usually do, the following, "Mrs. Smith, did you hear all the questions previously put to the jurors?" Her response was, "I can't do this. This is a man's job." The courtroom, already silent, got even more silent. I looked at counsel table and saw the United States attorney and the legal aide defense lawyer slump down in their chairs with their eyes cast to the ground as if to say to me, "She's all yours . . . " When I recovered, I said to Mrs. Smith, "Do you mean to say that you feel you could not follow the court's instructions as to the law applicable to this case?" And she said, "Yes, that's right." With that response, of course, she was excused for cause, as expected.

Very recently, my male hairdresser relocated to the staff of a beauty parlor in one of our major midtown department stores. He's a black man, and if you think the world has not changed, you should have been there in 1946 when I first started going to Lord & Taylor. They didn't have a single black sales clerk. And then they hired a black woman who looked like Lena Horne and they had her at the front counter as you entered the door, selling umbrellas. But if you go there now, you might even say black people own that store. When I went to this new location, my hairdresser and I witnessed the sexual harassment of a woman by another male hairdresser. They were standing next to us while he was trying to fix the door with a screwdriver for her. And as I've said, this took place right before us. My hairdresser said to me, "This goes on all the time." He said, as a matter of fact, the woman being harassed told him that she had been putting up with the harassment for 14 years—she'd been working there for 14 years. And I gathered from her appearance that she was a Pacific Islander. And I gathered from that 14 years, that the supervisor was probably aware of the conduct, but apparently had not done anything about it.

I think the women who are interested in seeing more women in public office or on the federal bench or liberated from on-the-job sexual harassment seem to forget that one of their enemies is other women. Other women who agree that women ought to be home in the kitchen. Other women who do not want to risk their careers by fighting for more women. Other women who fear retaliation if they file sexual harassment complaints. For example, we have four vacancies in our court in Manhattan. A full complement is now 28 judges. I was the only woman for 12 years. We now have 11 women, three of whom are seniors, like myself. And there will be four vacancies on the Court of Appeals for the Second Circuit when John Newman steps down in July as its Chief Judge after the Second Circuit Judicial Conference at Lake George. Maybe I've missed it, but I don't believe I've heard more than a peep out of any of the numerous women's bar associations on the issue of more women on the Second Circuit or the district courts. There's one black woman, as you know, on the Second Circuit, Amalya Kearse. She has publicly called for more women on that court. She did so last year in May when she was honored by the Federal Bar Counsel at the Waldorf Astoria. I believe she got the Learned Hand Award they give every year. She has been the only woman on the Second Circuit for the past 18 years. She, however, is passing up her chance to become the first woman chief judge of the Second Circuit when Newman steps down in July. Perhaps it is because women have made so much progress in the last 50 years in the legal profession that no one any longer sees a problem. However, the fight to abolish affirmative action for women generally, which is now sweeping the country, tells us that discrimination against women in employment may very well be a continuing problem in the future. All one has to do is to take a course in women's history to discover that the struggle for women's equality is centuries old, and to realize that the price of women's equality is eternal vigilance.

Karen Mathis
1998

6

Karen J. Mathis, a partner in the Denver, Colorado, office of McElroy, Deutsch, Mulvaney & Carpenter, LLP, is immediate past president of the American Bar Association. Ms. Mathis is a business, commercial, and estate-planning lawyer with more than 30 years' experience. Ms. Mathis earned her law degree from the University of Colorado School of Law. She has received honorary degrees from Siena College, the University of Denver,  *Michigan State University College of Law, Southwestern Law School, and California Western School of Law, and an honorary Order of the Coif from the University of Colorado. A member of the Colorado and International Women's Forums, Ms. Mathis has been honored as an outstanding lawyer by the Denver and Colorado Bar Associations, the University of Colorado, and the Albany Law School. An active member of the ABA for almost 30 years, Ms. Mathis served as the association's second-highest elected officer, chair of its House of Delegates, from*

Note: Following this Kate Stoneman address, Karen J. Mathis became the 130th President of the American Bar Association on August 9, 2006. She was the third woman to serve in the office and the first Coloradan to do so.

August 2000 until August 2002. She is the third woman to serve as an ABA president and the first president from Colorado. She has served as a member of the House of Delegates since 1982. Ms. Mathis is also a member of the ABA Board of Governors and has served on its Executive Committee, Operations Committee, and Program and Planning Committee. Ms. Mathis's extensive ABA involvement includes leadership of numerous ABA entities. She served as chair of the 30,000-member General Practice, Solo and Small Firm Section (now a Division) in 2002 to 2003; as chair of the Commission on Women in the Profession from 1997 to 2000; and as chair of the Standing Committee on Membership from 1994 to 1997. Ms. Mathis has also been active in the Denver Bar Association and Colorado Bar Association for many years. She has held offices in the Young Lawyers Section of both bar associations and served as vice president of the Colorado Bar Association from 1992 to 1993. Ms. Mathis has long been an advocate for our nation's youth, serving on the Colorado Commission on Child Care and as a member of the Mile Hi Council of Girl Scouts. She has spoken on five continents about the future of the law and women's place in the profession. She serves on the Advisory Boards of Martindale Hubbell and the Institute for the Advancement of the American Legal System. Her ABA presidential initiatives included Youth at Risk, Second Season of Service, Direct Women Institute, and Rule of Law.

I want to thank the committee that invited me and the three women who are so ably chairing the women's law caucus at this law school. Thank you to my friends, Patty Salkin, and to my handler today, another member of the Commission on Women, Nancy Hoffman, who's in the audience. It's a pleasure to be with all of you. And I want to thank you this evening for honoring me, but certainly, I more particularly want to thank you for honoring the work that the Commission on Women in the Legal Profession does through the American Bar Association. I know the commission is why I am here and, hopefully, it is one of the reasons that you're here as well. I am also very pleased that with us this evening is my law partner, Rosanne McCarthy Hall. Roseanne allows me the latitude and gives me the professional support to do the commission's work, including making visits like this to Albany. You know, Rosanne is very familiar with Albany Law School.

In fact, she grew up in Troy, New York. She has many associations with the area, and she was telling me that Ralph Semerad was the dean of your law school some 20 years or so ago. And, in fact, coincidentally, his daughter's name was also Dean. I understand that one evening his wife, Marjorie, a former Kate Stoneman recipient, answered their home phone and the caller asked for Dean Semerad. Marjorie then responded, "Dean doesn't live here anymore." I guess that the entire campus was quite abuzz the next day.

I would like to tell you something about the Commission on Women. Many of you have not had an opportunity to hear about its work or learn about its legacy. Our commission is appointed by the president of the American Bar Association. There are 12 of us, and we serve together with about 25 liaisons to do our work. During the past year alone our members and liaisons have visited more than 35 cities in 18 states, the United Kingdom, and Canada, talking about issues that are affecting women day-to-day in the legal profession. Those issues include the status of women in the legal profession, gender bias and gender-neutral evaluation in the workplace, gender equity in law schools, and best practices that affect lawyers in the profession. During those visits we have met with local state women's bar associations, with students, with deans, and with faculty. We have met with the judiciary. We have met with people in government and with countless women in all segments of our profession.

As I contemplate the importance of this celebration that we have today, and the woman that it commemorates, I think back to what it must have been like for Kate Stoneman, some hundred years ago. I understand she came from a hard-working farm family, the fifth of eight children. The gift her parents gave her, and that we can hope to give our own children, is one of access to books and to learning. She opted for a career in teaching, one of the few careers allowed to women outside the home at that time. Kate made that trip from Lakewood to Albany, New York, in 1864 in the middle of the Civil War. In the course of her 40-year career as a teacher, she used that platform as her beginning. She became interested in the suffrage movement and was politically active from the 1870s. Like Margaret Brent, another famous woman lawyer, Kate was named the executrix of a great aunt's estate over in Troy, New York. She was on her way on the road to law. I hope you all know Kate Stoneman's story. Judge Judith Kaye pointed it out so poignantly in her remarks a few years ago when receiving this award. Kate was the first woman in New York to become a member of the bar. After she passed the bar exam, she was denied admission by the New York State Supreme Court in 1886. But because of her political savvy and her work, she had her denial redressed by the state legislature within days. How easily that court dismissed her petition with these words, "no precedent, no English precedent, no necessity."

Today we're all beneficiaries of Kate Stoneman's legacy. As a lawyer, as a suffragette, as a feminist, and as an active supporter of world peace, she reflected in her life and in her actions the values the Commission on Women recognizes with its own annual presentation of the Margaret Brent Women Lawyers of Achievement Awards. These awards were established in 1991 to recognize and celebrate the accomplishments of women lawyers who achieve professional excellence in their field and influence other women to take on the mantle of the law; who open doors for women in nontraditional areas of the law; and who advance opportunities for women within their practice area. So, come back with me if you will, back to that woman, Margaret Brent, the first woman lawyer in America—back to 1638 in colonial Maryland. Margaret was very unusual. She came trained in the law and was a lawyer when she came to the colonies from England. She was a most unusual of colonists. She was educated. She was connected to royalty. Her cousins were Lord Baltimore and Lord Calvert. She became a large land holder. She was an advocate. She was a negotiator. Oh, and she was a woman. Like Kate Stoneman, Brent was tapped to be an executrix, in her case for her cousin, Lord Calvert, who died suddenly. And he was the governor of Maryland.

Over the next eight years, while she administered his estate, Margaret tried 124 cases and never lost one. How I wish I had that record. She'd frequently ask for jury trials despite the fact that by doing so she had to pay a tax of 15 pounds of tobacco per day per juror. Despite her name and her influence in the colony, she was turned down flat when she went to the Maryland Assembly and asked for a voice and a vote. She was, after all, only a woman. She continued as Calvert's executor. In fact, she quelled the first mutiny in the Maryland colony when she paid off the debts of Lord Calvert to his soldiers. And in the meantime, she had to slaughter both her own cattle and Lord Baltimore's, and he was decidedly unhappy about it. But she secured the peace of the colony. "Gentleman Margaret Brent" became her sobriquet. Hundreds of years later, Brent is commemorated in our commission's awards, while Governor Green, the fellow who agreed with the Maryland Assembly that she should not be given a voice and a vote, is a mere footnote in history.

We didn't start seeing women lawyers after Margaret Brent until the late 19th century. Belle Mansfield became the first woman admitted to the Bar in the U.S. in 1869, in Iowa. I hope that you'll have an opportunity to see the Commission's Trailblazers Exhibit downstairs, which talks about each woman lawyer in all 50 jurisdictions who was the first. More than a hundred years ago the United States Supreme Court, in considering petitions for women who were seeking the right to practice law, found that women's nature was unsuited to the profession. The decision read: "[women's nature] has essentially and habitually to do with all that is selfish and malicious, knavish and criminal, coarse, brutal, repulsive and obscene in human life." How much has changed?

But the times have changed since the 19th century. Recently, I attended the sesquicentennial of the Voting Rights Convention, which was held down the road in Seneca Falls in 1848, when Lucretia Mott and Elizabeth Cady Stanton and that wonderful abolitionist, Frederick Douglass, stood together with others to say that they found these truths to be self evident, that all men and women are created equal. No forces were strong enough to hold back the changes that were coming full force into American life. And of course on August 18, 1920, the 19th Amendment to our wonderful Constitution was ratified, giving women the right to vote for the first time. Remember, at that time, 100 years ago, women could not sit on juries. Women were not competent to be witnesses. Women could not be married and own their own property - just 100 years ago. While visiting our legal sisters in England last April, I was reminded that it took an act of Parliament in the year 1922 to allow women to become lawyers there.

So let's fast forward now to the 1970s and women in law schools. Women had been coming into the profession slowly in the 40s, the 50s, the 60s, but it really took the passage of Title VII to open the ivory towers to women students. And in the 1970s, it even took lawsuits to get the elite law firms to open their doors to women lawyers. In

1971 only 3% of the lawyers in this country were women. By 1980 that had risen to 8%, and to 16% in 1988. The most recent studies indicate that 26% of our profession is made up of women. From 1971 to 1991, there was a 16-fold increase in the number of women practicing law. You know, as the number of women increased in our profession, so did the number of women's bar associations. Today we even have a national conference of women's bars that works closely with the Commission, with state and local bars, and with women's bars, to work on these issues that still remain. In 1988, Hillary Rodham Clinton became the first Chair of the Commission I am now privileged to head. She submitted a landmark report to the American Bar Association assessing the status of women in our profession. That report predicted that time alone is unlikely to alter significantly the under-representation of women in law firm partnerships, judicial appointments and tenured faculty positions. To update that report we again went back and did hearings, focus groups, surveys, and studies. In 1996 this research was published in a book, "Unfinished Business: Overcoming the Sisyphus Factor." Do you all remember your Greek mythology - Sisyphus, forever pushing the stone up the hill, forever having it come back on him. The overall numbers of women in the legal profession have increased dramatically, but barriers can still persist. Discrimination continues to permeate structures, practices, and attitudes in our profession. Things like pay and equity, skewed opportunities for advancement, sexual harassment and hostility to family and personal needs continue to plague lawyers—not just women lawyers, but all lawyers of well-intentioned means.

We have made tremendous advancements. There are two women sitting on the Supreme Court. Two women have led the American Bar Association as its President and Chair of the House. To date, women comprised 31% of President Clinton's judicial appointments. There are increased numbers of women in law firms. Again, if you look at 1997, women were about 14% of partners in large law firms, compared to only 8% in 1988. In the judiciary, women representation has risen from 7% of the federal bench in 1987 to 19% in 1997. On our law school campuses, women are a significant force. Forty-five percent of all law students in this country are women. More than 12% of law schools in this country have 50% or more women in their student body. Still, less than 10% of the law school deans are women, and only about 19% are professors.

We know that there are issues. We know that there are problems. But as we like to say in the commission, we have admired the problems long enough and now we're ready to do something about them. The commission has continued to work with people like you, all over the country, to look at lawyering and balanced lives, to develop, implement, and draft policies that work for people who want balanced lives— "Fair Measure," which takes a look at the issue of gender neutral evaluation. Why do women come into law firms in equal numbers to their numbers in law school, but within five years you will not find them in the law firm? What is happening in this period of time and how can we help? Are women really not aggressive enough to be lawyers? Are women really too quiet? Do they really not care about their careers? We suggest that if you use a gender-neutral evaluation technique, then your firm, your law school, your government agency, your corporate office, will retain women and you will see women advancing. Studies such as "Elusive Equality," which examines the experiences of women in legal education and "The Burdens of Both, the Privileges of Neither," which has to do with multi-cultural women's experience in law school, are good beginnings. We have admired the problem long enough. What are we going to do about it?

We now have a booklet that's available, and I met with your dean and with people from the Student Bar Association and the Women's Law Caucus and other faculty members. Do a gender survey in your law school. Take a look at what issues might be out there that nobody has bothered percolating up. If there are any issues, then go about the work of addressing them. And if there aren't any issues, then publish it. Because not only will you find your women alumni giving more money to this law school than they have in the past, but you will continue to bring in the best students possible when they recognize that this is a place which is gender neutral and friendly. And finally, one that I love the most, is the whole issue of best practices. Do you know that 92 percent of law firms in this country have a flex-time policy? And yet only one percent of partners and only four percent of associates will use them? Gee, I wonder why.

So, how is our profession changing? Well, the demographics are changing. Since 1987, 37% of all people graduating from law school have been women. We now estimate from the Department of Labor that, by the year 2010, 50% of all lawyers in this country will be women and people of color. The demographics are changing dramatically. Law firms are telling us, "We want diversity." They're finally starting to say it. Why? Because their corporate clients are demanding it. And there's nothing more empowering than to see five general counsel sitting up on the dais, three of whom are women. There are companies like 3M and Dayton Hudson, saying, "We won't hire a firm that's not diverse." And suddenly, I'm hearing senior partners say, "How do we get diversity? We bring 'em in. We can't keep 'em!" We'll help you. We want to help you. We think that we're going to see some change in this area.

As I shared with some of you earlier today, there are a couple of issues that I'm seeing around the country that resonate for me and, I think, for many people. The young people I see in the law, whether they're students or just getting on to practicing say, "We want a balanced life. The practice of law is largely dysfunctional. Can't we be humanists and also be lawyers? And we want to do it, not men against women or women against men, but all together." And the answer is, "Yes, we can have balanced lives." An example: When I was in England, I found out that they'd done a survey of men and women lawyers. They found out that 90 percent of English male lawyers were parents. Only 40 percent of women in the law were mothers. Wouldn't it be interesting to see what the statistics would be in our own country? Because young women say to me, "Karen, I don't want you to be my role model. I don't want to live my life the way you did. I want to live it in a much more balanced fashion. And the law has to allow me to do that." If we work together, we can change some of those dysfunctional possibilities in a law firm or elsewhere.

I see affirmative action on the horizon as a major issue. The Commission on Women is going to work with the Commission on Minorities, with the ABA Individual Rights and Responsibilities Section, and with the Legal Education Section, to prepare and file an amicus brief in favor of continued diversity in law schools—and not let it be defined the way others want it to be defined as "affirmative action." We need diversity in our profession. At a time when we are more diverse than we have ever been as a culture, when within a few years, there will be more non-English speaking people than there are English-speaking people in the United States, we need diversity in our profession, or our profession will not have the impact that it has historically had in this country and throughout the world. For there to be more women professors on tenure track, there have to be more women who are given access to judicial clerkships. If you've seen what's been on the front pages of *USA Today* and what the Supreme Court of the United States has said or won't say about how it gets its law clerks; if you take a look at the number of women and also minorities; we are not doing a good enough job. Do you know that 40% of the clerks in the Supreme Court of the United States come from two law schools—Harvard and Yale? That's abominable! When they say they can't find people of color or women to fill these slots, well come on, folks, take off the blinders and start looking. There are more than 170 accredited law schools in this country, not just two. We have to do a better job.

I want to give you a few examples as we finish up today, of some current-day Kate Stonemans. The *National Law Journal* published for the first time a few months ago, what they called "Profiles in Power: The 50 Most Influential Women Lawyers in America." I don't know how many of you saw it. Out of 50, 14 of them hailed from your state, from New York. That's almost 30 percent of the most powerful women lawyers in the United States—and they're right here in your state. And that's not counting government lawyers or people who are on the bench—like your own, wonderful Judge Judith Kaye. Judge Kaye, I want to brag about you just a couple of minutes. Judith Kaye was called the "Mother of Justice" by an inmate, and I know from the inflection that person meant that as a compliment. She is the CEO of the vast New York judicial system. I had no idea—that's 14,000 employees! That's a billion dollar budget a year. That's 3.3 million cases out of 300 courts. That is astonishing! That is astronomical! That makes me tired! But what I really, really love about Judge Kaye is her heart. Her parents, Benjamin and Lena Smith, Polish Jews who fled persecution and settled in Monticello, New York, raised a daughter who believed in hard work, education, dedication, and the goodness of man and womankind. Judge Kaye is warm. She is generous. She remembers people with personal notes. Your state has been blessed with many wonderful people like Judge Kaye.

In the eight years that the Margaret Brent Awards of Achievement have been given, a number of them have been received by lawyers here in this state. And I just want to tell you a little bit about a few of them. Lynn Hecht-Shafran has been described as the Susan B. Anthony of our day. She's reasoned, empathetic, tenacious in her mission, and she's as convinced, as Susan was, that failure is impossible. She has worked tirelessly to eradicate gender bias in our legal system. And she has done it in many visages.

There is the second woman justice to the United States Supreme Court, Ruth Bader Ginsberg. She publicly defines, as a woman and a judge, the heights to which we can all hope to aspire. She's a scrupulous craftswoman. She supports women's rights. By her own example and her personal struggle, she has pioneered as a feminist in the legal profession. Betty Weinberg Ellerin, a founder of the Women's Bar Association of the State of New York, has striven for fairness to women litigants, for the protection of victims of domestic violence and the victims of child abuse.

And of course, the indefatigable and never to be forgotten, Honorable Bella Abzug. She was the first to vote for the Equal Rights Amendment. The first to introduce bills on child care, abortion rights, gay rights, and rehabilitation for Vietnam veterans. She was the first to dedicate women's concerns towards the saving of our planet. She was a civil rights and a labor leader throughout the 1950s and the 1960s. She defended the victims of racism and McCarthyism in this country. She led campaigns against nuclear testing and the Vietnam war. She was the first woman elected to Congress on the women's rights and peace platform. At one time, she was considered the third most influential member of Congress, and in 1977 a Gallup poll called her one of the 20 most influential women in the world. She was (the year before she received the Brent Award) inducted into the National Hall of Fame for Women in Seneca Falls.

As Hillary Rodham Clinton so eloquently said in her keynote address at the Margaret Brent luncheon a few years ago, "I want us, also, to be honoring the women who are struggling to hold body and soul together. Who are trying to do their jobs well and still make time for their families. Who want to do their work as best they can and still help their kids with homework. Who want to pitch in and help in their communities. Who want to be a friend to their friends. And maybe, most of all, they just want to take an afternoon off." Today is a celebration for each of us in this room and for all of those who are not with us. You should enjoy it. You should savor it. But I want you all to recall the words of Kate Stoneman in her last interview before she died at age 84. Kate said, "Time, place, and circumstances combine to help me accomplish my work." She encouraged young women to take their opportunities as they come, because always, there are opportunities to be had. I hope that you will join me, that you will join the Commission on Women, and that you will become a partner with us in our continued search for equality and fair play for men and for women.

Martha W. Barnett
1999

7

Martha W. Barnett is a partner in the law firm of Holland & Knight LLP and serves as chair of the Directors Com-mittee. Her primary areas of practice are administrative, governmental law, and public policy. Ms. Barnett has ex-tensive associations in the American Bar Association and The Florida Bar, including serving as president of the American Bar Association in 2000-2001. She also served as the chair of the American Bar Association House of  *Delegates, the first woman to serve in this position. Ms. Barnett served as chair of the Florida Commission on Ethics (1986-87) and a member of the Florida Constitu-tion Revision Committee (1997-98), the Florida Taxation & Budget Reform Commission (1990-94, 2007-present), the Governor's Select Committee on Workforce 2000, and the Florida Sales Tax on Services Study Commission (1986-87). Her additional affiliations with the American Bar Association include serving as a member of the Ex-ecutive Board and as chair, since 2006, of the Central European & Eurasian Law Initiative (CEELI); as a past member of the ABA Board of Governors; and as a life member of the House of Delegates. Ms. Barnett is a mem-ber of the Board of Administrators at Tulane University;*

the American Law Institute; and the Legal Advisory Board of Martindale-Hubbell/LexisNexis. Her numerous awards include The Florida Bar Association Medal of Honor (2002) and National Woman of Distinction by the Girl Scouts of the USA (2002). Ms. Barnett presented the Preiskel-Silverman Lecture on "Terrorism, Technology, and the Changing Reality of Personal Privacy" in 2003. Her extensive professional honors include receiving the Distinguished Alumnae of Tulane University Award (2001), the University of Florida Distinguished Alumnus Award (2006), and being named one of "Florida's Legal Elite," selected by the state's attorneys and published in Florida Trend *magazine (2005-07). Ms. Barnett is a graduate of Newcomb College, Tulane University of Louisiana (B.A., cum laude, 1969), and the University of Florida (J.D., cum laude, 1973), where she served as editor of the University of Florida Law Review.*

PIONEERS OF THE NEW AGE

I'm honored that Judge Kaye is here and it's nice to see old friends and to meet new friends. I want to take just a minute and acknowledge the reason I'm here. It has little to do with the fact that I'm president-elect of the ABA and everything to do with one of your graduates, who is also my law partner and friend, Dianne Phillips. I want to say what a privilege it is to know Dianne. I'm here to honor her and bask in a little of her reflected glory.

It is a pleasure to be in upstate New York, at the Albany Law School, and a privilege to deliver the Kate Stoneman lecture. My firm recently published a wonderful tribute to me as its first woman lawyer and the president-elect of the ABA. I was very pleased—and more than a little proud. Whatever firsts that I—and so many in this room have—pale in comparison to Kate Stoneman's accomplishments. She was the first woman lawyer in New York and did so much to open doors and create opportunities for the rest of us to walk through.

In the last year, I have spoken several times at events honoring women lawyers. Wisconsin's sequescentennial celebration of its statehood honored its first 150 women lawyers. Just last week, the Minnesota Women Lawyers established the Rosalie Wahl lecture in honor of Justice Rosalie Wahl, the first woman on its Supreme Court, and the other pioneering women lawyers: Nevada, Utah, and other states have done something similar. Millennium madness? Maybe. But I like it. It is very important. It is a time to remember our history, celebrate our successes, and commit to our futures.

We always talk in terms of numbers. "Firsts." First woman; first 50; first 100 women; first 100 years. Behind those numbers are stories—rich stories of women who made a difference. Just last year, Albany Law School celebrated Kate Stoneman's graduation 100 years ago. A century has passed. A long time? I guess it is if you are a 15-year-old longing for that driver's license, but, we grown-ups know it is but a moment in time. It is remarkable what has happened in the short span of a century. Even more remarkable when you remember that women could not go to college, could not be a doctor or a lawyer, could not keep our own earnings, could not marry if we were teachers, could not vote—until 80 years ago!

Happily, things have changed and now with critical mass, the rate of change is escalating. New York has more than its share of women who are agents for change. Chief among them is Judith Kaye, the Chief Judge of New York. She is one of my heroes. Her accomplishments are legendary! Just this past week, she was honored by the Center for State Courts with the William Rehnquist Award for Excellence for the innovations she has implemented in the court system in this state, from drug courts, to domestic violence courts, to commercial divisions, to foster cost-effective dispute resolution in business deals. In her acceptance remarks, Judge Kaye said that there is a crisis in the public trust and confidence in all public institutions, including the justice system. I am told that she keeps a portrait of Justice John Jay over the bench in her chambers. She has fulfilled his admonition that "next to doing right, the great object in the administration of justice should be to give the public satisfaction." Judge Kaye, the first woman to serve on the New York Court of Appeals and as its chief, deserves our gratitude.

She is not alone. Chief Judge Kaye is joined on the bench of New York's highest court by her colleague, Carmen Beauchamp Ciparick. Judge Ciparick is an important role model for all Americans, but especially for women of color.

The judiciary does not have a monopoly on well-known and accomplished women. The lieutenant governor of New York, Mary

Donohue, a lawyer, is a past member of the New York Supreme Court and a district attorney of Rensselaer County. There is rumor of another accomplished and well-known woman lawyer seeking to represent New York in the U.S. Senate. These women just show that Kate Stoneman knew that she changed the law and opened the first door for women lawyers in New York.

There is another equally important reason that this is an appropriate venue to celebrate accomplishments of women. Upstate New York is the birthplace of the women's movement. Last year marked the 150th anniversary of the first Women's Rights Convention held in Seneca Falls, less than three hours from here, at the tip of Lake Seneca in the beautiful rolling hills of central New York. But, of course, you all know this—better to have someone else brag about them. So for all of these reasons, from Dianne Phillips to Judge Kaye to Seneca Falls, I am honored to be with you to share some of my thoughts tonight.

We can't rest on our laurels or take for granted the progress that has been made. A story reported by Barbara Walters is illustrative. She had done a series on gender roles in Kuwait several years before the Gulf War, and she noted then that women customarily walked about 10 feet behind their husbands. She returned to Kuwait recently and observed that the men now walked several yards behind their wives. Ms. Walters approached one of the women for an explanation. "This is marvelous!" she said. "What enabled women here to achieve this reversal of roles?" The Kuwaiti woman replied: "Land mines."

Tonight, I want to look to the future and focus on the responsibility that those of us in leadership have to ensure that future for the next generation. A lot has happened since Kate Stoneman and Seneca Falls. We are living in a dynamic world. Change is all around us and we need to learn from it and capitalize on it. For example, in the next century, which is just 44 days away, people of color will become the majority in our country. One of the most dramatic demographic changes, of course, is the increased participation of women in leadership positions.

Great leaders and institutions are already figuring out how to use these demographics to their advantage. They are not just recruiting and hiring minorities and women, they are integrating those individuals into the structure of their institutions. It is not a coincidence to me that one of the American Bar Association's primary focuses now is increasing diversity in the profession. We have seen the future. We know what our society will look like, and we believe that the justice system at every level must reflect the makeup of that society. It is also no coincidence to me that my law firm, a firm of more than 900 lawyers, has a Minority Initiative, and a Women's Initiative. They are part of our effort to make sure that the firm is positioned for the next decade and the next century of opportunities that we hope will come our way.

Evidence is everywhere. Available data shows that women between the ages of 25 and 35 are better educated than the men in this same age group. More associates, bachelors, and masters degrees are being earned by women. Women now earn about 40 percent of the PhD's and make up about 46 percent of entering law school classes and 42 percent of entering medical school classes. The 1999 entering law school class of Boalt Hall, the law school at the University of California at Berkeley, was 59 percent female. I understand that for several years more than 50 percent of Albany Law School's student body has been women. The same statistics are reflected in the other professions, whether it's medical or accounting or otherwise.

There are changes, occurring at the top, as well. My current position in the ABA is but one example. Judge Kaye's position as chief judge is another. Similar changes are occurring in business. New businesses are started by women at a rate double that of men. Even in large established businesses, women are increasing their presence in leadership and management roles. Since 1993, the percentage of *Fortune* 500 companies with women on their boards of directors has increased from 69 percent to 86 percent. (That 14 percent still do not have women is shocking!)

Carleton (Carly) S. Fiorina, the new CEO at Hewlett-Packard, has become the symbol of the shattered glass ceiling. The hiring of a woman to run one of the largest corporations in the world, and a technology company at that, made headline news. What is even more telling is that, according to published reports, at least two of the four finalists were women.

In the 26 years that I have been practicing law, I have seen many changes in the legal profession and in my own firm. I was the proverbial first woman. Looking back, I think it was probably more traumatic for the law firm than it was for me. But, they handled it fairly well, and we all survived and even thrived, hopefully because of it.

Several years later I had occasion to look at my personnel file and there was my resumé, complete with several notes stapled to it. I couldn't stand it—I had to look at what someone thought was important enough to attach to my resumé when I was interviewed. One attachment was a copy of a newspaper article about a large international law firm in New York City being sued for "sex discrimination" (this was even before "gender" was the politically correct term). The other was a handwritten note from the associate that reviewed resumés for the firm's recruiting partner (and a former law school classmate). The note said, "If we have to hire a woman, let's hire this one."

Today, my firm hires as many women as we do men. Smart companies, and I like to think we are one, go beyond the numbers, however. They implement institutional changes that reflect, indeed promote, the changing face and color of business. For example, we emphasize our commitment to diversity. We try to move to a higher level of professional services by incorporating the opinions, the ides, the visions and the solutions that come from a diverse workforce. We view diversity as a competitive edge. In fact, we try to capitalize on it with programs such as those I previously mentioned, a "Minority Initiative" and a "Women's Initiative." We have a marketing slogan that proclaims, "At Holland & Knight, Women Mean Business." Of course, these initiatives send the not too subtle message that the firm views women as serious professionals. But more importantly, it recognizes—and advertises—that women are sources of new business, and that we are the next generation of rainmakers.

I have two children, a son and a daughter. Feminist that I am, as committed to equality as I am, it did not take me very long to understand what I had always known: girls and boys are different—really different—thank goodness! I celebrate our differences.

I want to make it clear; I like men—a lot. I married one of them. Male colleagues have been allies and have been essential in opening doors for women. I would not be where I am today had it not been for the tutelage and tenacity of my firm's senior partner.

But the most sympathetic and sensitive man, no matter how hard he tries, cannot see through a woman's eyes or hear with our ears. This should not surprise anyone. Our Hispanic and African-American friends tell us that every day. Our experiences are different; our perspectives are different; we come at issues from different places; we process information through a different filter. We govern, manage, and solve problems in different ways. Those differences make a difference. It is not just a numbers game. It is not just the right thing to do. It is the smart business thing to do.

Happily, the pipeline is full of qualified, seasoned women who are ready for those opportunities. Women no longer are simply reaching for entry into the mainstream; we are the mainstream. But—there is always a but—with success comes responsibility. It is important that women now use their special skills and unique experiences to shape the future in a way that we think is appropriate. Now that women have some power, let's change the way power is used.

What are some of the things that we can do; indeed, what are some of the things we must do? Mentoring, philanthropy, and using power to effect change are three that I think are very important.

Mentoring

The importance of this cannot be overstated. It is essential. Whatever success I have had, I attribute, in large measure, to the tutelage and vision of my firm's founding partner. His role in my life was captured a number of years ago in an article about future presidents of the ABA. In talking favorably about my prospects, the reporter attributed it to the fact that I had Chesterfield Smith "at my side, by my side, and on my side." A good mentor is one who opens doors for you, then steps aside and lets you walk through. Each of you should be a mentor. Pick one of the many law students here tonight. This is a good way to ensure the success of the next generation and of our profession. Reach out and I guarantee that you will make a difference not just in their life, but also in yours.

Philanthropy

Historically, women have been reluctant to write checks although more and more women have access to large amounts of money. That is changing. Emily's List showed us how successful we could be in the political arena. More universities, law schools, foundations, and charities are looking to women for significant contributions. I serve on my law school's board of trustees. Many of you do the same. More and more, institutions are reaching out to women for the first time to contribute, not just their time, but their dollars. Community service is another type of philanthropy. It is just as important, and will help secure the freedom for the next generation.

Use Power to Effect Change

Perhaps this is the most difficult, but also the most important of all. The one that I think is the most interesting is now that there is a critical mass of women in leadership roles, how do we use those leadership roles and the power that comes with them in a constructive, effective way to make significant changes? Of course, it has already happened. What used to be dismissed as "women's issues"—equal pay, health care, education, family leave, family values—are now the issues of the day. It is no coincidence that this has occurred as the numbers of women in positions of power in business and government have reached an all time high.

I recently addressed the National Association of Women Judges at their annual meeting in Miami. Consistent with their theme, "New Faces of Justice," I focused my remarks on the newest, most innocent faces of all—our children. I want to share some of my comments with you as I believe this is an area where we can effectively use power to effect change, not because women have a monopoly on the subject. We don't. It is because there is a crisis in the juvenile justice system and we have a special interest, if only because of our traditional unique role. This is one of those times where we see these issues through different lenses. It is also one area where women with power can use that power to make a real difference.

Too often our children are forgotten, neglected, and rejected, first by their families and then by our society. As lawyers, as judges, especially as women, we have an obligation to make sure the justice system does not reject them. These children deserve a future, not only for their sakes, but also for ours. If anyone thinks we can ignore these newest faces in the justice system, just remember the recent incidents of troubled youths gunning down their classmates and teachers. Schools, however, are actually among the safest venues. The chance of a student being killed in school is, literally, one in a million. Yet, as a direct consequence of gangs and guns, 40 kids each week are killed and 98 percent of youth murders occur outside of school.

Let me provide some perspective on how serious this problem is. Since the Littleton shootings in April, almost 2,000 additional young people have died from gunshot wounds in our country. Approximately 12 die every day from a combination of intentional shootings, accidents, and suicide. This tragic loss of life is an epidemic. It is far worse here than in any other developed nation in the world. The U.S. has the highest rate of overall gun deaths for children under 15 years of age, higher than the 25 other industrialized countries combined.

Juvenile offenders present the largest problem facing society and, likewise, the justice system. The juvenile justice caseload is increasing at a dramatic rate. According to the National Center for State Courts, in 1997, the most recent year for which it has data available, there were just over 2 million juvenile filings in state courts. This represents a 70 percent increase in little more than a decade. This is a much more rapid rate than the general criminal and civil caseloads.

One trend that is becoming increasingly clear and that is particularly troubling, is that young girls are entering the juvenile justice system at very high and increasing rates. At a time when the world is opening up for women, it is tragic that our daughters are increasingly involved in the justice system in ways that we cannot countenance.

Another disturbing trend is that we are sending an increasing number of juveniles—of both genders—to the criminal justice system to be treated as adults. The Center on Juvenile and Criminal Justice just completed a study on the so-called "Florida Experience" that raises substantial questions about the wisdom of allowing prosecutors—rather than judges—such authority.

One example is illustrative. Tony (not his real name) is the kind of kid who has never been a danger to anyone. A 15-year-old eighth grader with an IQ of 58, he is described as having the mind of a 5-year-old. Last year, shortly after his mother died, Tony asked another boy in his class at a Florida middle school to give him lunch money, claiming he was hungry. When the boy refused, Tony reached into the boy's pocket and took $2. That's when Tony ran smack into the county prosecutor who declared that he had a zero tolerance for this type of activity. Rather than handling the case in the principal's office where it belonged, he prosecuted Tony as an adult for this, his first arrest. He spent the next seven weeks, including his first Christmas since his mother died, in custody, much of it in an adult jail. Tony was just one of 4,660 youths Florida prosecutors sent to adult court last year under the wide-ranging powers they enjoy with the state's direct file provisions. Florida is one of 15 states where prosecutors, not judges, decide whether children arrested for crimes ranging from shoplifting to robbery should be dealt with in the criminal justice system or in the juvenile justice system. As a lawyer, this bothers me. As a parent, this bothers me.

A juvenile crime bill currently being considered by the U.S. Congress would give U.S. attorneys even greater powers than those enjoyed by Florida prosecutors. The change in federal law would remove judges from the process of deciding which justice system would serve young people, and transfer that power to the sole discretion of prosecutors. The ABA opposes this legislation and is lobbying Congress to draft this proposal.

If the Florida experience is any indication, there are problems in the future. Here are some findings from the Florida study:

- Most juveniles treated as adults are charged with nonviolent property offenses.
- The recidivism rate of those children is higher than those in the juvenile justice system.
- Despite the prosecutor's discretion, the Florida crime rate has stayed above the national average.
- Children face much higher risk of physical harm in adult detention centers than in juvenile detention.

Proposed solutions for addressing the rising rate of violent juvenile crime range from fully funding Head Start programs, to additional authority for juvenile judges, to more effective gun control.

Let's talk about gun control for a minute. Where I come from, talking about gun control ensures that you will never be elected to public office. There has been a concerted effort to delay any further action. As of today—almost one year since the Columbine shootings—the conferees appointed in July, have not even met and it is unclear even if they will meet before the end of this session of Congress. I do not believe that we can allow this opportunity to be squandered. Congress should act now to close the gun show loophole. We know this is one way that teens get guns. Data has been collected as part of the federal Youth Crime Gun Interdiction Initiative, a program that originated in Boston, and which has been expanded to over 50 large cities nationwide. It traces every gun used in a crime by youth back to its origin of sale and supports prosecution of gun traffickers who supply these guns to individual youths and gangs. These are modest reforms. Data collected through this tracing show that gun shows are the leading supplier to criminals and youth. The shooters at Littleton got two of their guns from gun shows, including a high-powered military assault weapon.

It is ironic that in 1999, as we debate whether to treat our youth as adults in criminal court, and to limit access to firearms by children, we also celebrate the centennial of the juvenile court in America. This is a natural opportunity for all of us to take stock of where we are and to reflect on where we need to be. The unique and special nature of the problems of children in the justice system reaffirms what has been evident for at least 100 years. The special needs of juveniles require that special services be dedicated to children. As I started out, this is one area where we can use the power and confidence that comes with our new roles as leaders and take care of these newest faces in our justice system.

If you will indulge me for a few more minutes, I would like to close with a personal story about an important woman in my life who taught me a lot of lessons. I grew up as the daughter of what is today known as an ol' country doctor in a small town in rural Florida, a thriving metropolis of 500. There wasn't a lot to do and hunting and fishing were favorite past times. My father and brothers loved to hunt, but it was my mama who was the fisherman in our home. She loved to fish, particularly for bass. Mama, like most fishermen, was always trying to catch what she called the Big One.

I remember many a late night, Mama and several of her other women friends coming home with their string of fish, proudly showing off their catch. I'd ask, "Mama, did you catch the Big One tonight?" She'd say, "No, Martha, not tonight." "But Mama, that's a pretty big bass," I'd respond. She'd allow how that was true, but say she felt this might be his brother or maybe his cousin or one of his children, but not the Big One. Although Mama fished almost all her life, I don't think she ever caught that big bass, but she never stopped trying.

I have thought about my mother and that big bass over the years, beyond any reference to fish or fishing. No matter how good a person does, how well he or she succeeds, she never achieves the perfection she wants. A lawyer may get a good verdict in a hard case, but a really good lawyer always knows he or she can do better the next time. Leaders must recognize that there are always new avenues to explore. We never really catch the Big One, but we ought to keep trying and keep the feeling, indeed the hope, that we just might do it the next time.

So it is with each of us. As far as we have come, as successful as women have been in achieving leadership in the new age, my challenge to you—in the spirit of Kate Stoneman and in the spirit of a new millennium—is to at least keep the feeling, indeed preserve the hope, that we just might do even better.

Notes

1. Centers for Disease Control, Rates of homicide, suicide, and firearm-related death among children—26 industrialized countries (1997). Compared to these 25 other industrialized countries combined, the U.S. overall gun-related death rate is 12 times higher; the gun homicide rate is 16 times higher; the gun suicide rate is 11 times higher; and the unintentional gun death rate is 9 times higher.

2. HOWARD SNYDER & MELISSA SICKMUND, JUVENILE OFFENDERS AND VICTIMS: UPDATE ON VIOLENCE (Washington, D.C.: Office of Juvenile Justice and Delinquency Prevention, 1998).

3. VINCENT SCHIRALDI & JASON ZIEDENBERG, THE FLORIDA EXPERIMENT: AN ANALYSIS OF THE IMPACT OF GRANTING PROSECUTORS DISCRETION TO TRY JUVENILES AS ADULTS (July 1999).

Hon. Mary O. Donohue
2000

8

Hon. Mary O. Donohue is a judge for the New York Court of Claims and a former lieutenant governor of the state of New York. She was first elected as  *lieutenant governor in 1998 and was reelected in 2002 on a ticket with Governor George Pataki. In 1999, Governor Pataki appointed her to chair the Governor's Task Force on School Violence. During her tenure, she also chaired the Governor's Task Force on Quality Communities and Task Force on Small Business. Additionally, the lieutenant governor promoted criminal justice reforms, including anti-terrorism, DWI, drug, and DNA legislation. In 1996, Lieutenant Governor Donohue was elected to the State Supreme Court for the seven-county Third Judicial District by an impressive 20,000-vote margin in a six-way race. Prior to her service as the first female State Supreme Court Justice from Rensselaer County, the lieutenant governor was elected as Rensselaer County's first female district attorney in 1992. She was reelected in 1995 with an unprecedented 70% of the vote. During her tenure as district attorney, she achieved convictions in over 90% of the criminal justice cases she handled, including domestic violence, child abuse, elder abuse, and juvenile justice.*

She personally tried cases ranging from murder and attempted murder to sexual abuse, all of which resulted in convictions, and oversaw nearly 5,000 criminal prosecutions each year. Prior to her government service, Lieutenant Governor Donohue was a teacher and an attorney. She is a graduate of the College of New Rochelle, Russell Sage College, and Albany Law School. During law school, she served as a law clerk and intern in the U.S. Attorney's Office in Albany and worked on the staff of New York Senator Joseph Bruno.

I am indeed privileged to join you this evening to be your keynote speaker and to receive a prestigious award, an award that means the world to me. I receive many invitations to be keynote speaker around the state, as you can imagine, and many of them I don't see personally. This was among them. In the spring one of my staff mentioned, "Oh, you've been asked to be keynote speaker at the Kate Stoneman day." I said, "Oh, wonderful. I definitely want to make that a priority." It was in June, Mimi, when I was with you at Whiteman, Osterman & Hanna at breakfast, that you said to me how happy you were to see me receiving the award. Did you notice the change in my face? It was at that moment that I realized, "Me? Receive the Kate Stoneman award?" I didn't say anything to you, because I didn't want to be presumptuous. I thought, well, I'd misinterpreted, and I called my office for them to check that letter. What else did it say? Of course, my staff knew. They thought they would surprise me with it, but I think my reaction at the moment that you made me aware of that said something about the value and the great reverence I have for this award. I've been here each year seeing and sharing the delight of celebration with the award winners, and of all of the occasions of my career I say to you that this moment, being here with you to receive this award from my alma mater, means a tremendous amount to me—perhaps more than any other recognition I've received in my career.

It's always a pleasure for me to come back to Albany Law and to celebrate tonight the achievements of women, particularly women lawyers. Congratulations to the other award recipient, Martha Davis, who is at Albany Law as the first Kate Stoneman endowed visiting professor in law and democracy. My alma mater is certainly fortunate to have the benefit of your experience and insight this semester, Martha.

Kate Stoneman's legacy is one of courage, determination, confidence, and conviction. Our founding fathers and mothers had great faith in the idea of self-rule and the irrepressible spirit of the individual. They demonstrated that faith by building the foundation of our free society, which would empower people to express their own ideas and to choose their own path in life. Unfortunately, nonetheless, in the infancy of our democracy those freedoms were not extended to everyone. It took people like Kate Stoneman, Harriett Tubman, and Martin Luther King, Jr., to achieve equal rights for all. These individuals and many others like them fought for our equality, redefined our democracy, and, in fact, achieved the truest meaning for that time-honored phrase, "We hold these truths to be self evident, that all men are created equal." It was the very concept of freedom which enabled pioneers like Kate Stoneman to persevere and to fight for the rights which we so richly enjoy and too often take for granted today. It is astounding when one considers the events that have led to our ability to gather like this in celebration this evening.

I would like to take a moment to recount a few of the more interesting and formidable obstacles faced by the first women lawyers. In South Carolina, Ms. James Perry was a woman with a male name, so she was off to a good start, I guess, in terms of the fight she had ahead. She moved to California from South Carolina to earn her law degree, and she practiced there for several years until her home state finally passed a law in 1918 permitting women to join the bar. In opposing the bill, one very self-expressed, learned South Carolina assemblyman (did you get that intonation?) stated that, and I quote, "It was unjust to the men that women should enter into competition with them." He believed, perhaps with some reality, that the chances of his sons, who were studying to become lawyers, would be significantly lessened by having women in the profession.

Lest you think that California was a bastion of women lawyers, the story of Clara Shortridge Foltz tells otherwise. In 1874 Clara, then a teacher in Illinois, moved with her husband and five young children to California. Soon afterwards, she and her husband divorced, and she began teaching because she was the full support of her family. When her interest turned to law, she applied for several apprenticeships with lawyers, all of whom were male. Only one—but on the positive side it only took one—lawyer did give her the golden opportunity to be an apprentice. After developing a solid reputation as a trial lawyer she sought admission to law school at Hastings. Her application was summarily denied on the grounds that, and I quote again, "The rustling of her petticoats would distract the students." End of quote, but not end of story, fortunately. That didn't stop her. Clara attended classes at Hastings until the janitor literally threw her out. He had more power than she did. Two years afterwards she was admitted to the California Bar, and then the California Supreme Court held that Hastings could not deny her admission based on her gender. Although she had won her case in court, she still did not receive a degree from Hastings until 1990, when Hastings conferred her with an honorary degree.

As evidenced by these few stories, we have made quantum strides for equal rights. We must be proud of the women who, like Kate Stoneman, have carved a path for women lawyers like many of us today. We must not take our freedom for granted, however, as there are still many more milestones ahead for us. Upstate New York is the birthplace of the Women's Rights Movement. Did you know that Elizabeth Cady Stanton was born and bred the daughter of a lawyer in Fulton County, right in our backyard? Very sadly, I didn't know that until two years ago when we celebrated the 150th Anniversary of the Women's Rights Movement, although I was educated in Rensselaer County and Albany County, right near Fulton County. This alone shows how many milestones we have made just in our own lifetime, in our own adulthood. I encourage you to study the historical contributions of women in our State, across the country, and around the world to fully appreciate the import of the freedom and the opportunities which are available to women because of those early pioneers. I believe we are keeping alive and well the tradition that was started 152 years ago in upstate New York by Elizabeth Cady Stanton and Susan B. Anthony, as exemplified by our gathering here this evening and many other examples from day to day, particularly here in Albany.

My belief in the power of the individual has been a principal which has guided me throughout my life—the principal which has helped me develop and helped me attain my goals and many of my dreams. Yes, I have been a teacher, a lawyer, a district attorney, a judge, and now your lieutenant governor, but the most important and fulfilling title I will ever have is that of Mom. I look out and I see Professor Stevenson. I remember when I was a student here, the joy of celebrating with you the birth of your daughter; and how often when I was in law school I thought at the time—am I doing the right thing? My daughter was 11 months old when I took the law boards. I recall that it was a very, very difficult decision and time in my life.

I was raised in a very traditional, Irish Catholic family in Troy, New York. I was the daughter of, yes, a lawyer and a judge. I was the sister of, yes, a lawyer. I then became the wife of, yes, a lawyer, but, "Who, me? Do that?" The answer to myself was always negative. In the way that I was raised it was always my belief, because my first priority was to raise a family, that I wouldn't have time for anything else. When I graduated from the 8th grade at Sacred Heart School in Troy, the class prophecy was that I would be the first lady judge in Troy. Well, Judge Griffin, you're ahead of me, but I was the first lady judge from the city of Troy. When that prophecy was made, I came home and said to my parents, "Can you believe that? I would never do that, because I would never have time for that in my life."

That prophecy showed that some perhaps knew more than I did along the way. After I had been teaching for a decade, I took a leave as a tenured teacher and then had my daughter Sara in '78. Over that next year she was a good baby, and I kept looking at her and thinking, "I think I can go to law school." Nonetheless, in terms of my traditional family and my traditional beliefs, which I still have tremendous respect for, the answer would still have been no. Around that time I recall making my daily visit to my mother, an old-fashioned Irish matriarch. That day I said to her, "Mom, I'm taking the law boards." Sara was there, just sitting up at ten months, when my Mother said, "This is a disgrace, and if she were old enough to talk she'd tell you just what she thought of you." Strong, independent minds go way back in my family! I said to her, "Mom, you always taught me to do what I believed was right. Now I'm a mother. I have to do what I believe is right to set the example for her. I can't just do what you believed was right for you, so I will take the law boards! I have to find out if the congenital family defect is in me." For better or worse, there it was. I applied to several law schools and was accepted at law schools out of this area. I discussed with Professor Welsh at the time my decision to stay here and to go to Albany Law, because that was where I drew the line. I believed that it would be right for me and for my family for me to go to law school, but to travel a distance would have been too much for that little baby who meant more to me than anything in the world. Of course, now Sara says to me, "You stayed in Troy for ME?" I say, "Yes, and I have no regrets." And why would I? Look at how good my hometown and my home area have been for me and my family. It certainly was a good decision.

I started law school at age 33—just about everyone else was 23 or younger! I believe I was the only freshman in that class who was going home to change diapers with a baby who was still a toddler. So I'd be home changing diapers and hardly managing to get to class. Where's Professor Moriarity? I think I made it all but two or three times, didn't I? I recall toward the end of the first semester sitting next to a young woman in Professor Wallace's class when it got to be like boot camp here with the grind before exams. I would study maybe two hours if I could after Sara went to bed around 9 or 9:30 p.m., thinking "Gee, this is going great." I was living and breathing it, and I loved it. I'd been out of school so long, and it was wonderful to be here. Then this young woman leaned over to me in class and said to me, "Do you take breaks for meals?" That's when I realized: what have I gotten myself into? This is what I was competing—I shouldn't say, against, because they became my friends—but that's when I started to worry.

Fortunately, God was with me, determination was with me, belief in my power as an individual was with me. It was a success for me, and I did graduate. In law school I was working two jobs at one point. I was on my own as a mother and taking care of Sara, but I just believed that this was the best thing to do.

After I graduated I was blessed to get a job at O'Connor & Aronowitz, and my mother and I had never discussed the "L" thing from that first day. We were still very close. After I'd been at O'Connell & Aronowitz about six months and was the only woman in the firm, I was still trying so hard to do my job as professionally as possible, sometimes maybe trying too hard and too sternly. One day in that time period, I came down I-787 from Troy in a snowstorm and arrived at work to find Neil Murray at the door. I was handling the Dalkon Shield cases for the firm and was waiting for a big decision from Brooklyn regarding whether equitable estoppel would apply to give us a chance to go to bat for these victims. He was all smiles, and I said, "We won, didn't we?" He said, "Well, I'll tell you about that later." What he wanted to tell me with a laugh was, "Your mother called. She wanted to know if you made it through the storm." I was so humiliated, but, you know, that broke the ice with Neil Murray and all the others in the firm a lot more than any other work that I could have done for the firm. Yes, by the way, we did win the motion in Brooklyn.

I learned something from that incident, although that day I was so infuriated with my mother for calling like that I drove home straight to her apartment and said, "Mom, how could you have done that to me?" She said, "You're still my child. You always will be and I have something to tell you." I didn't know then, but maybe she knew then. She was ill, and she died not long after that, within a year, but she looked me straight in the eyes in her strong Irish way, the story of women in my family, and said to me, "You know, Mary, you were right to go to law school. It's obvious that you're fulfilled, Sara's doing great, and, I don't know how, but it seems to make you happy. Of course, it's not anything I would ever have done, God knows, and I still think you should have just been president of the auxiliary."

Well, I always respected those choices that she had made. I think it's important to observe that many of my friends from the class of '68 at the College of New Rochelle have never worked. Some of them have chosen to work part-time. Some of those women who made those choices are the brightest women I'll ever know. Law school was the choice that was right for me, not necessarily anyone else. That's the important point: the power of the individual choice.

Along the way there were challenges, many more challenges than in law school. I always look back on law school as the bright, salad days of my intellectual pursuits: a wonderful place to be prepared for the pit, as I believe I was well prepared here at Albany Law. I recall a law firm meeting with my male attorney colleagues that was held at the Fort Orange Club in the fall of 1983. Then, of course, no women were members at the club. As I walked in, I experienced something unlike anything at Albany Law School. We were in a Utopia here. Everything was nongender here, and I say this spontaneously: what a rude awakening I had that day. One of my male colleagues said to me, "Mary, take a good look at these walls, because the only way you'll see them is when you're here with me." That was 1983, a reminder of how far we have come just in a span of my short professional career.

I decided in 1988 to open up my own law office after the birth of my son (I have a 12-year-old son, Justin). I enjoyed practicing law with a firm, but I always had wanted to start my own office. To make ends meet, I also became assistant county attorney. In 1992, there was a contest for the district attorney position involving a challenge to a sitting DA who was an ex-FBI agent. At that time there was no female county-wide, elected official, and the DA's office had always been a traditionally male bastion. Many people encouraged me to run, saying; "You're a trial lawyer, and you wanted to go into public service." That is why I went into law school, ironically. I'd been involved in many community service pursuits before law school. My dream was to come back to my hometown and to be in community service. That was the chart I had been mapping out.

I did decide to run, but I thought at the time that it was going to be perhaps the biggest challenge of my career. Many other people thought I would be a sacrificial lamb! That was not for a minute what I had in mind, although along the campaign trail there were some really rude awakenings. I recall an incident which stands out always in my mind when I think of gender discrimination. It's when I realized how much it hurts, how much people are hurt by discrimination, whether it's on the basis of gender or any other immutable quality. I was campaigning then with Judge Hummel, who is still Family Court Judge in Rensselaer County. He and I were a good campaigning team. I was making a reservation for a chicken barbecue, and I said to him, "I saw in the paper a notice for the PBA (Police Benevolent Association) dinner. It said anyone who wants to attend should call this number." He said, "Fine, I'll get those reservations: You'll take care of something else." We had a lot to do that day, so he made two reservations for the PBA dinner. I happened to mention that to someone who said, "You're going? Don't go." I said, "Why not?" He said, "Because it's male only." I said, "It's for professionals who work with the police. I read it in the paper. I prosecute juveniles for Rensselaer County. I handle all their civil litigation. I handle all their criminal work. I work with the police, day in and day out. I'll call the president of the PBA. I'm sure there's some misunderstanding." The PBA president said, "Don't go," when I called him. I asked him why, and he said, "Because you're a woman. It's a stag event, only for male professionals who work with the police." So I responded, "Okay, Jack, I'm running for DA. I'd like the PBA endorsement." I wanted to think globally here—the negotiator in me! "I want an interview. Will you give me an interview? Maybe I'll just stop by at the cocktail hour." He said, "Sure, sure, but you're not invited to the cocktail hour." I didn't want to stay for the whole dinner anyway, to be perfectly honest! So I waited—no interview occurred. The next week I read in the paper that they had endorsed my opponent. They had invited him to the PBA dinner.

Then, I had a very difficult decision to make. I was wounded. I had never experienced anything like that, and I do believe it was blatantly discriminatory. I sat in my office and thought, "What do I do?" Do I polarize this whole campaign over gender discrimination and allow that be the whole theme? Do I keep sight of what the battle is, and see what happens? I decided the way for me to win that battle was not to polarize the whole campaign and distract from the issues. I was concerned about plea bargaining. I was concerned about a lot of things going on in the DA's office that I wanted to deal with on a substantive level as a campaigner. So, I let it go. Other people heard about it, and there was quite a bit of negative reaction to it. I decided the way for me to deal with that issue was to win in November, because I knew that the sitting DA always sat at the head table at the PBA dinner every year! So, the day after the election (this says something about me; I have to admit I relished this), I called Jack, the PBA president, and said, "Hi, Jack, it's the DA-elect. Get that tablecloth cleaned, because next year I'll be there at the PBA dinner, sitting right next to you." And I was. He has always worked with me in a very professional way. I think he was afraid, as were some other individuals, that I would want retribution. No, no, because I knew that it wasn't the rank and file who decided to exclude me. It was more of a political decision, maybe, I'd like to think, than a gender-based decision.

Do you know what I found as the first female DA in Rensselaer County? As a candidate, I'd received none of the endorsements, absolutely none of the endorsements. Nobody thought I could win. I went to the people, as an individual, all over. As a candidate I was everywhere talking about what I wanted to do and the difference I wanted to make. I never discussed gender. I've always believed in running on my credentials and running on the substantive issues. Of course, making history as the first female DA is something that definitely gets my adrenaline going and definitely something I'm very proud of—but it should always be a priority for all of us as female professionals to achieve based on substance, not based on gender. So, as the first female DA, I had many concerns. Even some of my friends who supported me had said, "You're not going to try murder cases, are you? No female here has ever tried a murder case." This was true in the Capital Region, astoundingly, eight years ago. But I did. That's one of the reasons I wanted to be DA. I wanted to try those murder cases. As a friend of mine had said on the campaign trail (he was a banker), "I'm going to support you. I'm a liberal Democrat, but I believe in you. I don't think you have a chance, because you don't have the power. You don't have the old boys' network behind you." Every time I see him he visibly shrinks because he accused me of being powerless eight years ago!

I think the message has to be that it's not the power structure. It's not the gender. It's reaching out to the people and having the power of the individual perseverance. When I ran for re-election I received the PBA endorsement, and I also received every endorsement that was given because of the substance of what I had done as DA. That meant the world to me. Also, when I was re-elected I had the honor of making history with the largest margin of votes, not as a female but as a DA, in the history of Rensselaer County. The people responded to the work that I had done on their behalf.

I felt very settled as a DA in my second term when I was asked to consider running for state supreme court. At first I said, "No, I've had two campaigns in the last three years." Then I thought of my own goals and how much I truly did want to be on the state supreme court bench. I had the delight and honor of running with Judge Victoria Graffeo and Judge Mizelle. Vicky, I'm sure you recall that incisive interview with Alan Chartock, of course, live on T.V., where he sprung the question to the three of us: "Do you think you do your jobs differently as women?" That was the question I'd been trying to avoid, zealously, my whole career. We talked about it, my running mates answered in the negative and it then came my time to answer. I knew as a DA that who I was, and what my gender was, was a part of the person I was as DA. I said without hesitation, "There's no question. We do do our jobs differently as women, but not necessarily better."

Now, as your lieutenant governor, I think it's so important that, regardless of our gender, we bring our gender to what we do without focusing on it, as a part of who we are. Otherwise, how will we represent all of the individuals in the state of New York? It's important to be comfortable with ourselves wherever we go. The path I took has not always been easy, but certainly it's been rewarding, and it's been far easier as I look back than I could have dreamed.

I want to quote, in closing, Teddy Roosevelt's words that have meant quite a bit to me over my years—not only in public service but my years as a professional. He once said:

> It is not the critic who counts, not the man who points out how the strong man stumbles or where the doer of deeds could have done better. The credit belongs to the man who is actually in the arena, whose face is marred by dust and sweat and blood, who strives valiantly, who errs and comes up short again and again, because there is no effort without error or shortcoming, but who knows the great enthusiasms, the great devotions, who spends himself for a worthy cause, who, at the best, knows, in the end, the triumph of high achievement, and who, at the worst, if he fails, at least he fails while daring greatly, so that his place shall never be with those cold and timid souls who knew neither victory nor defeat.

Before I finish, I do want to tell you that in the last year I spoke on this topic with my daughter, Sara, who is now a college graduate working in Manhattan, working hard, playing hard, making choices that maybe I wouldn't have made. See, I'm sounding more like my mother every day! As I told her, I do worry. Did I make the right decision? This IS what it's all about—our future, our children, others' children, the next generation. I asked her, "Sara, do you remember when I'd take you to law school and you'd sit in the library and read those books?" I thought at those times: "Oh, she's getting all this intellectual stimulation." Linda Dwyer, do you remember Sara being here with us sometimes? Well, she said to me last year, "Mom, to be perfectly honest, the only thing I remember about Albany Law is the ice cream machine in the cafeteria." I guess you can't achieve all your goals! She also said to me, "Why do you ask? Do you have any second thoughts about what you did?" I said, "I only would if you feel that you fell short, or I fell short as your mom, because of it." She said, "Mom, every step of the way you've been my inspiration, and you always will be." There was only one person missing from that conversation: my mother.

This is the story of three generations of women in my family. It's crucial that we each choose the path that follows the beat of our own individual hearts. I hope that my story encourages all of you to believe in your talents, your skills, and your goals, to believe in your valued self. Be the person in the arena. Have the courage to take chances and to make mistakes. Heaven knows, I've made my share! Remember the impact of Kate Stoneman's achievements on all of us. Create your own individual legacy in the image of Kate Stoneman. Always remember that one woman can, without question, make a tremendous difference in the long haul, as Kate Stoneman has for each and every one of us here this evening.

Hon. Mary Jo White
2002

9

Mary Jo White is a partner with the law firm of Debevoise & Plimpton. Ms. White served as U.S. attorney for the Southern District of New York in January 1993-2002, where she was acclaimed as the leader of what is widely recognized as the premier U.S. Attorney's Office in the nation. She has supervised over 200 assistant U.S. attorneys in successfully prosecuting some of the most important national and international matters, including complex white-collar and international  *terrorism cases. Ms. White is the recipient of numerous awards and is regularly ranked as a leading lawyer by directories that evaluate law firms. In addition, Ms. White served as a director of the Nasdaq Stock Exchange and on its Executive, Audit and Policy Committees (2002 to February 2006). She is also a member of the Council on Foreign Relations. When Ms. White rejoined Debevoise in 2002, she was made chair of the firm's over 225-lawyer Litigation Department and has been ranked in the top tier among the leading "Litigation: Trial Lawyers" by* Chambers Global The World's Leading Lawyers for Business *(2006). Ms. White's recent representations of public record include HCA in the Department of Justice and SEC insider-trading investigation of Senate Majority Leader William Frist. She is the only woman to hold the top position in the U.S. Attorney's office in the more than 200-year history of that office, which has the responsibility of enforcing the federal criminal and civil laws of the nation. Ms. White has received numerous awards and honorary degrees for her professional accomplishments, including the George W. Bush Award for Excellence in Counterterrorism and the Agency Seal Medallion given by the CIA. From 1983 to 1990, Ms. White was a litigation partner at Debevoise, where she focused on white-collar defense work, SEC enforcement matters, and commercial and professional civil litigation. From 1978 to 1981, Ms. White served as an assistant U.S. attorney in the Southern District of New York, where she became chief appellate attorney of the Criminal Division. Prior to that, she worked as an associate at Debevoise from 1976 to 1978. Ms. White served as a law clerk to the Honorable Marvin E. Frankel, U.S. District Court for the Southern District of New York, and was admitted to the bar in New York in 1975. Ms. White graduated from William & Mary College, Phi Beta Kappa, with a B.A. in psychology in 1970; The New School for Social Research, with an M.A. in psychology in 1971; and Columbia Law School, with a J.D. in 1974, where she was an officer of the Law Review.*

It is indeed my pleasure and honor to speak to you on this very important day at Albany Law School—Kate Stoneman Day. I'm going to begin my remarks by reading, just very briefly, two sentences from that old statute that brings us here in some ways. It reads, "The race or sex of such person applicant shall constitute no cause for refusing such person admission to practice in the court of record of this state as an attorney or counselor. This act shall take place immediately." So read the May 19, 1886, revision to Code 56 of the New York Code of Civil Procedure that changed history and the life and lot of professional women in the state of New York. The "such person" who forced this short but ground-breaking statutory amendment was, of course, Kate Stoneman, the woman and heroine of our profession whose legacy we celebrate today.

As all here know well, Kate Stoneman was a strong woman, a strong person, who, after passing the New York state bar exam, refused to take no for an answer and persuaded the state legislature to change the law to permit her to become the first woman to be admitted to our bar. That was 116 years ago next month. It would be over 30 years after Miss Stoneman became a lawyer that women won the right to vote, after a very long and difficult struggle, in which Miss Stoneman also played a significant role as secretary of the Women's Suffrage Society of Albany. But 20 years before Kate Stoneman was to see the vote for women become a reality and 12 years after she was admitted to the bar, she was to achieve another major milestone, as all of you know, by becoming in 1898, at the age of 57, the first woman to graduate from this fine law school. And I think it is particularly fitting that Kate Stoneman attended and earned her L.L.B. degree from Albany Law School, which since its founding in 1851, has recognized the value of experience in legal practice as well as legal theory. How appropriate a choice in venue for Kate Stoneman, who although without doubt, highly intelligent, and well educated in both law and the liberal arts, was above all a doer. A teacher, a practicing lawyer, a suffragette, an active and unwavering champion of so many important issues of her day and ours. It was she who said at the age of 84, just before she died, that aspiring women must, "take their opportunities as they come. Always there are opportunities to be had." That is what Kate Stoneman said in 1925.

So, how well have we done by the year 2002 in following Kate Stoneman's advice and her call to us to seize our opportunities? Where do professional women, lawyers and others stand today? What have we achieved? How far have we come? What is left to be done and how do we get there? In the legal profession that Kate Stoneman pioneered for women, we have witnessed, and there is no other word for it, a sea change of progress and accomplishments since 1886. A true revolution, as Supreme Court Justice Sandra Day O'Connor calls it. For nearly three quarters of a century after Kate Stoneman graduated from this law school and practiced law in this state, women who attended law schools were few and far between. To say that they were outnumbered in the law schools and the legal profession would be a massive understatement. For many, many years the number of women in law school classes across the country was one or two or none. And those few who did graduate and become members of the bar found doors closed to them at every turn. And even if we bring ourselves forward in time to 1952, the year Sandra Day O'Connor graduated from Stanford Law School, the picture for women lawyers was not a bright one. Although Justice O'Connor graduated at the top of her class and was a member of the law review, she was unable to get a job at any national law firm except as a legal secretary. Why? One reason only—she was a woman. And in the view of the marketplace, women, even those who graduated from law school at the very top of their class, really belonged at home and not in the serious legal workplace, which was, as late as 1952, still and stubbornly reserved almost exclusively for men. Now, I have to say, it's almost impossible for me, a law school graduate some 20 years after Justice O'Connor, let alone for many of you of more present day vintage, to even relate to the overt discrimination that women lawyers faced in 1952.

Today the picture is much brighter and the numbers are impressive. Women are now over 30 percent of the lawyers in the United States. We are well over 40 percent of the law graduates. When I graduated from Columbia Law School in 1974, there were 45 women in my class, 17 percent of the class. In 1999 there were 153 women graduates at Columbia, 44 percent. In many law schools, including yours, women number over 50 percent of the students entering in graduating classes. Twenty percent of the nation's judges are now women. About one quarter of our United States attorneys have been women in recent years. Almost 50 percent of the starting associates in large New York City law firms are women. Nearly 15 percent of the partners are women. The percentage in 1980 was 3 percent. So, by the numbers, women have achieved a lot in the profession that Kate Stoneman broke the barrier to in 1886. But it is not just the overall numbers that show the progress of women in the legal profession. The positions women now occupy are also at the very top of our profession. In 1981, as we all know, Justice O'Connor became the first woman justice on the Supreme Court. She has since been joined by Ruth Bader Ginsburg as her associate justice. Associate Justice Ginsburg was actually a professor at Columbia Law School when I was a student there in the 1970s. Judith Kaye, who is with us, a prior recipient of the Kate Stoneman Award, is our esteemed chief judge of the state's very highest court. Professor Katheryn Katz of the class of 1970 and Gloria Herron Arthur of the class of 1985, both prior recipients of the Kate Stoneman Award, respectively, the founding partner of the first women-owned law firm in Albany and the first African-American partner in a top 10 law firm in the Capital District. We have now had our first woman attorney general and deputy attorney general of the United States, as well as the first woman secretary of state. Barbara Jones, who is here today, is now a United States District Judge in the Southern District of New York. She was also the first woman to ever serve as chief of an organized crime strike force in the United States Department of Justice. Women occupy top general counsel positions in major corporations and they are deans of law schools. On a more mortal level, I have just completed a nearly nine-year tenure as the first woman to serve as United States attorney in the Southern District of New York. And, as you heard, just last week I returned to Debevoise & Plimpton, where I began my legal career as a summer associate in 1973 and was actually the second woman partner at that firm in 1983 and I am now the chair of the litigation department which has over 150 lawyers.

There are countless other examples, obviously, of women firsts in the legal world and in nearly every other profession. The number of women CEOs in major companies continues to grow, as do the number elected to public office. Just last week, you may have seen it, there was an article in *The New York Times* entitled, "In 2002 woman's place may be, not in the kitchen, but in the State House." The article reports on the increasing number of women running for and winning a national political office. Today, 10 percent of the state governors are women, 13 percent of the United States senators are women, 14 percent of the members of the House of Representatives are women. Dramatic increases compared to 10 years ago. Impressive? Yes, absolutely, yes. But the numbers also show how much remains to be achieved. Why are only 13 of 100 United States Senators women when over half of our adult population is female? Why no woman president or vice president or chief justice of the Supreme Court? We obviously have more miles to go on that road Kate Stoneman helped get us started on in 1886. What we are seeking of course, is the day that it is no longer news that a woman has been appointed or elected to any high position. The focus should be on the person and his or her qualifications, not on gender. And this business of numbers and women firsts, I think can be and is often overdone sometimes. But we should also not get too comfortable with our successes and the comparative increases in the numbers. Some absolute numbers are important if women are to have equal opportunity in all of the professions. As Justice O'Connor has said of our legal profession, "Until all of the percentages come close to 50 percent we cannot say we have succeeded." She is right.

The numbers and percentages do matter to how much clout and comfort we have in any given professional setting. They also matter as to how attractive a particular profession or job setting will be to other women making career and life choices. I think the most dramatic illustration of this point for me came early in my tenure as United States attorney, when I was also serving, as you're heard, as the chair of Attorney General, Janet Reno's, Advisory Committee, which consisted of 21 U.S. attorneys from all over the country, and its function was to advise the attorney general on various matters of policy. In my capacity as chair, I traveled to Washington, believe it or not, one morning a week for over a year, to attend the attorney general's weekly executive staff meetings. These meetings were attended by all of the top Justice Department officials. The solicitor general of the United States, obviously the attorney general of the United States, the deputy attorney general and all of the assistant attorneys general in the department, about 25 to 30 people in all. Most appointed by the President of the United States and confirmed by the senate. A pretty heavy duty group as groups go. And I think for the very first time, in fact I know for the very first time in my own career, the women in this high-level, high-powered setting, outnumbered the men. And I don't think it was my imagination—I'm certain it wasn't my imagination—that the men in this unfamiliar environment, were somewhat chilled and reticent about expressing their views and making arguments, while the women were patently more comfortable and spoke up more freely. In other words, the atmosphere and professional climate were defined, at least to some extent, by the relative number of men and women at the meeting. Now this may seem obvious, but at least for me it was a revelation of sorts, I have to confess. Maybe we women have been outnumbered for so long in power settings that we just don't consciously think about it or the impact that it may be having on us. But the imbalance in the numbers is a reality that continues to exist and operate on us in ways that, I think at least, are not conducive to optimal performance and success. So, we must continue to strive for greater representation for women in these power settings and all settings in the legal profession. Women first are important, but they are just the beginning.

One of the biggest challenges in the 21st century for women may be to redefine what the relevant marks of success and professional achievements are and should be. It may be that at least a part of the glass ceiling women face is of our own making because we may too readily accept the goals and definitions of success handed to us by a society and professions historically dominated by men and their aspirations and values. Women should not aspire to positions, lifestyles and jobs just because we may have been subjected to unfair and discriminatory barriers in the past. We should strive for things because we genuinely want them. We should also work toward redefining success and how to get there. And the same goes for ideas, causes, interests, and points of view. There are many things on which most women do and, I think, should agree. Equal pay, equal health care attention, equal professional respect and opportunity. But there are many things and many issues on which our gender should be irrelevant and no indication whatsoever of what we think, believe, care about or want to achieve. There is obviously no such thing as a single set of points of view that all or most women hold. Some of us favor the death penalty, others are against it. The same, of course, is true of men. Some women are for gun control, others are against it. Some favor raising taxes, others don't. Some women, like some men, are pro life, while many others are vigorously pro choice. The point is that women are individuals and we must resist every effort to be stereotyped, either as to what opinion we hold or should hold or as to what job we can have or should want to have. We need to be and feel free to be ourselves and to be judged and treated as the complicated individualists that we all are. We also need to avoid setting goals for ourselves because women haven't been there before, only men have. I for one, at least, do not seek for women to become 50 percent or 51 percent of every grouping or every profession. For example, I have no aspiration for women to become 50 percent of the convicted felons in our jails. Nor do I have an aspiration necessarily for them to become 50 percent of our jailors. And I think it is a good thing, a very good thing, that women are woefully underrepresented in the domestic militia movements that seek to bring down our government.

Women, I do believe, bring unique perspectives and dimensions and insights to issues and problems. We don't want to lose those unique qualities that can affect such positive societal change in the hunt for professional equality and success. We should later rest once and for all the tired adage for success for women published in *Fortune* magazine in 1990, which was (we know it, many of us), "Look like a lady, act like a man, work like a dog." Hopefully, today's version of that advice at least reads this way, "Look like you want to, act like yourself, and work like a dog." Two out of three . . . we may not get rid of the last one, I don't know. What we want the 21st century to be is as close to a ceilingless century as is possible to attain for women and men to have equal opportunity, equal pay and the freedom and acceptance to be themselves without confining stereotypes that either limit us or define us. What is today regarded as success in the legal profession is expanding and diversifying. Women, in particular, I think, are taking the lead in redefining success. Money, positions of traditional prestige, partnerships in large law firms, are not the only or even primary yardsticks. Overall job satisfaction, public service, and a more sensible and satisfying balance of our professional and private lives are growing in importance as the barometers of success for both women and men. These are positive developments, but we must keep striving. We must also do everything we can to help other women coming behind us to enter and succeed in the legal profession at every level.

Achieving equality for women in any aspect of our society has never been easy, just ask Kate Stoneman. But the outlook is good and we should be optimistic about the future. And as we strive for equality for women in the legal profession, I cannot think of a better role model than Kate Stoneman, whose life and courage constitute the best evidence of what women can and have achieved, and against much greater odds and barriers than any of us face today. She achieved all that she did by being herself and by being true to the person that she was and wanted to be. She would not take "no" for an answer when the answer should have been "yes." That is her message to us in the year 2002, the message to us, women and men. If we follow it there is absolutely nothing that we cannot achieve.

Carol Dinkins
2003

10

Carol Dinkins was nominated by President George W. Bush and in February 2006 confirmed by the Senate to chair the newly formed Privacy and Civil Liberties Oversight Board. A partner at Vinson & Elkins, she chairs the law firm's administrative and environmental law practice. She handles all aspects of client counseling on business transactions and permit matters, as well as civil litigation, mediation, and criminal defense. Ms. Dinkins has represented chemical and energy companies,  *developers, timber, utilities, transportation interests, and a variety of municipal and governmental entities in proceedings under state and federal environmental and natural resources laws. She maintains offices in Houston, Texas, and Washington, D.C., and has served on the firm's Management Committee. From 1981 to 1983, Ms. Dinkins served as Assistant Attorney General in charge of the Environment and Natural Resources Division of the Department of Justice, where she supervised the government's litigation in federal environmental, natural resources, and Indian and public lands cases. In 1984-1985, she served as Deputy Attorney General of the United States, the second-ranking official in the Department of*

Justice. Her responsibilities included working with members of Congress, the White House, the cabinet, and subcabinet officers on policy, legislation, and litigation. Her extensive experience at the law firm includes serving as lead negotiator to resolve a case involving characterization and remediation of PCBs and other substances at 60 sites in over a dozen states and half a dozen EPA regions, as well as numerous other environmental litigation and settlement, permitting, and counseling successes. Ms. Dinkins is listed in The International Who's Who of Environmental Lawyers *as among the top 18 environmental lawyers in the world and the only one listed in Texas. A small sample of her affiliations are: American Bar Association, member, Board of Governors (2005-2008); chair, Standing Committee on the Federal Judiciary (2002-2003); member (1997-1998), House of Delegates; member, Nominating Committee (1998-2005, 1994-1997); chair, Rules and Calendar Committee (2000-2002), member (1996-1998); chair, Board of Editors,* ABA Journal *(2003-2007), member (1998-2007). She is a former chair of the Board of Directors of The Nature Conservancy. Ms. Dinkins graduated from the University of Houston Law Center, J.D., 1971 and the University of Texas, B.S. Ed., 1968.*

It is an honor to be recognized with the outstanding women receiving the Kate Stoneman award this evening. Thank you, Patty Salkin, for bringing me to the attention of your Kate Stoneman Committee, and thank you, committee, for bringing me to Albany and this fine law school.

Kate Stoneman first became known to me when Karen Mathis and Martha Barnett were honored with this award, of which they're very proud. Viewing the tape of the wonderful tribute to Ms. Stoneman given by Chief Judge Judith Kaye is an inspiration in itself. Kate Stoneman's observation that "Time, place, and circumstances combined to help me accomplish my work" beautifully recognizes the human factor—the people who encouraged, mentored, coached, championed, recognized my opportunities and helped me to become and to be a lawyer—it describes my career path. I was invited to spend these minutes sharing some of my history—telling some of my story—but I do so with the caution that it is far more difficult to speak of one's self than of the complexities of Section 404(b)(1) of Public Law 92-500.

Perhaps some of my experiences mirror yours, or you will find encouragement for or suggestions to help with advancing your own goals in what I have to share. I will touch only briefly on a variety of matters and hope one of them will speak particularly to you.

Kate Stoneman came from a farming family. Judge Kaye pondered whether her having an old law book, perhaps one of very few, if any other, books, led her to the law. Although mine is a family largely of farmers, my father is a lawyer. At 79, he still practices law; my mother drives him to court regularly in the county seats around my home town. They argue and bicker all the way to court and back, but we did celebrate their sixtieth wedding anniversary this past weekend.

One day doing the dishes when I was in the eighth grade, Mother asked what I wanted to do and I said be a lawyer because Dad spends his time reading, writing, and talking to people and that's how I like to spend my time. She did not discourage me, although neither of us knew any women lawyers. I went straight from college to law school and even though my first daughter was born the intervening summer, my mother didn't say "why don't you stay home with that precious baby." However, my paternal grandmother said, "This is good because you and her father can take turns going to class and tending the baby," which we did.

Today I will cover just a few topics—presidential appointments, building a national practice, volunteer activities, and the final topic, but never the last priority—raising children while building a career.

Presidential Appointments

The most coveted presidential appointments are PAS—presidential appointment with senate confirmation. I had two in the Reagan Justice Department. I wanted the first because I'd been a partner for a year and was ready for a new challenge; because you cannot learn in Houston in private practice what you can sitting in the seat of a high-level federal official/decision-maker; because during the campaign, President Reagan was criticized on conservation and environmental matters, and I thought my experience could be helpful to his administration. And not least, I did it because I could.

What can you learn? How the decision and policy-making occurs at the highest levels in Washington; what the process is; who the players are; how the agenda is set, changed, not met, or achieved. How to distinguish real players from those at the margins.

What did I like? Having a place at the table in national policy-making and debates. Making a difference in federal litigation results. A number of my division's cases went to the Supreme Court; we won one of them 5-4 only because I successfully argued with and convinced the Solicitor General and the Secretary of the Interior to seek certiorari. I still treasure the dear friends I made among my fellow appointees and the career people at Justice who are such very dedicated public servants.

What did I not like? The vitriolic nature of some partisan politics. The unavoidable reality that some people in positions of power are bullies. Being caught up in a Congressional and then independent counsel investigation. I spent all one day testifying before a D.C. federal grand jury. It may be a character-building experience, but I already had as much character as I wanted.

The three of us caught up in this investigation challenged the constitutionality of the independent counsel law, since allowed to sunset, all the way to the U.S. Supreme Court. Just last month Harvard law professor and former Solicitor General Fried said he'd just taught our case in one of his courses.

Why did I go back into the government as deputy attorney general? Because I could. Because when the attorney general first offered the position and I demurred, he said, "You can't turn this down." He was right. Because this is the second-highest ranking law enforcement official in the world. Because I liked the attorney general and my other colleagues so very much. Because it was another opportunity to learn and do things not possible in Houston, Texas.

What did I learn? About foreign counterintelligence, surveillance, FBI training, and preparedness. This position is so neat—holding it so exhilarating—that I cannot capture it, only give a few illustrations. I was among about eight lawyers who joined the President for tea at the White House with the Supreme Court Justices on the Thursday preceding the first Monday in October. When the attorney general was out of town, I attended cabinet meetings. The attorney general always sits to the left of the vice president. I have a handwritten note that then-Vice President Bush passed to me during one cabinet meeting asking if I'd like a ride home on *Air Force Two* for Christmas. I went undercover with the FBI, on night operations at Chula Vista with the border patrol, and night operations on an aircraft carrier, staying in the quarters of the Admiral of the Fleet. When the attorney general was recused on a case, I met with President Reagan and the secretaries of state and defense in the Oval Office because as acting attorney general, I made a decision to take an action that Secretaries Weinberg and Schultz entreated the President to countermand, which he did.

Hopefully, I've piqued your interest in presidential appointments, so how do you get one?

First, you should have suitable experience and background and a good reputation in your field. Almost always you should at least not have been a contributor to the other political party and its candidates. Ideally, you voted in the last party primary. The rest is good timing, good coaching, well-regarded and effective champions, and, most importantly, good luck.

For my first appointment, one coach was also my mentor at my law firm; another coach was a young lawyer/special assistant to the then-governor of Texas; my champion was the governor and former governor. The governor was my champion because of my success at pro bono work in chairing his Task Force on Coastal Zone Management, writing the program and negotiating preliminary federal approval.

If you aspire to a PAS, find a coach and identify some champions. You cannot assume these would be the head of the office of presidential personnel or the President. No, you need someone whose primary mission is you. You may find a coach who is recruited by one of your colleagues at your firm or school or a client. You may need help identifying your champions, but you must know them personally, although their active support can be enlisted by someone other than you. This discourse isn't meant to be a primer; its only intent is to apprize you of a need to know enough to seek help. The rest will be on-the-job training.

National Practice/National Reputation

Government service has been a defining part of my career, and it contributed significantly to my building a national practice and achieving a national reputation. But you need not be a public official to develop a national practice and reputation.

How do you build one? What does it consist of? It is one in which you work outside your state and region, with law firms and governmental entities in other states. But a national practice essentially is one that involves significant issues and entities.

How do you get this business? Who sends it? Often times these are referrals from other law firms, lawyers whom I knew in the government, or lawyers whom I have come to know through my American Bar Association activities. How you develop a national practice is a question the answers to which must be tailored to the practice area and the people. Mine is an outgrowth of having been in government service and knowing environmental lawyers all over the country through public speaking and organizations. The downside of a national practice is the travel, although that also is an appealing part of it. However, staying at a Motel 6 because it is the best available, sleeping bolt upright at SFO at midnight awaiting a red-eye flight, flying middle seat coach, unfed, overnight from Anchorage does reflect the true "glamour" of the situation.

Professional Organization Activities

Another area that I would like to address is that of professional activities. How does one advance in this area? By being available for assignments and by treating those assignments and deadlines as though they were billable work. You must perform or you won't be asked to serve in other positions nor will you be advanced to leadership roles. You must show up for similar reasons. You cannot miss a lot of meetings and expect to be regarded as a player. In the ABA, just as anywhere else, having mentors, coaches and champions is a key. I have been very fortunate in that regard. My predecessor as chair of the State and Local Government Law Section knew that the section would have a much-coveted, three-year position on the ABA-wide Nominating Committee and he urged that I take that appointment, which I did. He then coached me on assuring that candidates asked for my vote and that I understood what kind of policies they would follow if in office. That kind of mentoring gave me an insight into what I would have to do to be effective and I was able to capitalize to the point where, in the first two contested races where I had a vote, one of my candidates won by one vote and the other by two. They then gave me appointments to good ABA positions. I try to use my being very well-connected and really visible in the association to help the entity I represent and others to get appointments.

Volunteer Work

Moving from professional organizations to governmental, nongovernmental (NGO) and other volunteer activities, I want to make a pitch for you each to have this as a personal objective going forward. Just as ABA service is an opportunity to give back to the profession that rewards us so well, volunteer work of all kinds is an opportunity to give back to the community and to do something for the public and the future. I choose to volunteer my time for conservation activities and to the Houston Museum of Natural Science. Serving as vice chair of the Texas Parks & Wildlife Commission, a gubernatorial appointment with senate confirmation, meant that I was a state official. The commission regulates hunting, fishing—commercial and recreational—non-game species, endangered species and, of course, the state parks.

My Nature Conservancy volunteer activity also will last far into the future. The conservancy has a plan for what is needed to protect the most biologically diverse and important areas of the country, Conservation by Design. Working in a focused way, both state and nationally, being part of this organization really gives a sense that it is possible to assure the diversity of plants and animals we enjoy today will extend generations into the future. I am the only lawyer on the national board of governors; many other members are CEOs of *Fortune* 500 companies.

Leadership

Now I want to urge you to aspire to be leaders, to chair entities and not just be a passive member. Why would you want to do this? Because if you are the chair, you can set the agenda, you can set the style, you can set the priorities in a way you never can if you're only a member. There is a cost, of course. You cannot miss the meetings; you spend considerably more time than does just a member; you are more open to criticism; and, if you are unsuccessful, you are responsible for the organization's setbacks or failures. On the other hand, if you work hard, are focused and goal-oriented, you can enjoy the reflected glory of the organization's success. More importantly, you have the satisfaction—and it is immense—of knowing that you have made a difference.

What do you do to get to be a leader? A chair not just a member? The same way as I described advancement in the ABA. You have to work hard; you have to show up at meetings; you must have a commitment and even a passion for the mission of the organization. In other words, you must demonstrate leadership potential and interest. But, beyond that, you need the support of and, again, to be championed by the right people and you need to be regarded as someone who can set an agenda, can fulfill the mission, knows how to set and achieve priorities, can run a meeting with a courteous but firm hand, and can recruit help and inspire others to devote time to the organization. Again, you work at these efforts just as hard as you do your client work for which you are paid. The pay, of course, is far different. If you choose the right organizations, you have the opportunity to make a lasting difference. You need not campaign to be elected or selected to chair an entity, but you must show that you can do it and sometimes you need to say that you want to do it. You also must be very sure that it fits into the rest of your schedule because I have not yet found a chairmanship that was undemanding. It probably would have been unsatisfying.

Family

We come now to the last point on my list for today. And that is raising children while building a career. I have two daughters, one born the summer between college and law school and the other born the summer that I graduated law school and took the bar exam, right before I started my first job as a lawyer. Why did I have children at such an early age? Because I could. Because I wanted to. Because I thought it would work best to have children in their infancy and youth while my career was in its infancy and youth, so that we all could grow together. It worked for me and more importantly, for them. Well-adjusted. Married. Very close. Nannies didn't manifest themselves until I was long past needing one, but household help and childcare was essential. I didn't find it possible to do anything but practice law and raise children when they were young. You can't expect more. All my outside activities centered on them—teaching Sunday School, organizing a Brownie troop, car pooling soccer teams, chaperoning weekend field trips. When I was in the government, my family stayed in Houston and I commuted every week to Washington. My daughters came up in the summer and have a great grounding in government and American history because of all the sightseeing they could do in the time they spent at the department with me. When I was deputy attorney general, my younger daughter called my office one afternoon because she was working on a paper and she wanted to interview a high-level government official about the death penalty. We talked about this for a few minutes and then she sprang the question, "So, Mom, could you call Justice O'Connor and ask what she thinks?" I thought an interview with the deputy attorney general was sufficient and declined to make that call for her.

In reflecting on how to balance a family with the very time-consuming practice and outside activities I have had, my best advice would be that your spouse and children also enjoy travel—if you travel in your practice—and the kinds of activities you enjoy. I have been remarried for six years, and my lawyer-husband loves to hunt and fish, is an ardent conservationist, and enjoys my ABA friends. If that were not the case, I wouldn't participate in so many activities because it would take me away from home without him far too often.

Conclusion

It both astonishes and bemuses me that a century after Ms. Stoneman's great successes there remained so many firsts for a woman lawyer. I've watched a great many and achieved some—first woman partner in a major Texas firm, first woman on the Management Committee, first woman section head, first woman assistant attorney general of the Environment and Natural Resources Division, first woman deputy attorney general. Everything requires time, hard work, and help.

Thank you for this kind invitation and this great honor, and all the best wishes to each of you in your own careers and pursuit of your outside interests. May you find it all fun and fulfilling.

Professor Herma Hill Kay
2004

11

Herma Hill Kay is the Barbara Nachtrieb Armstrong Professor of Law at Boalt Hall, the University of California-Berkeley School of Law. Following law school, Professor Kay was law clerk to Justice Roger Traynor of the California Supreme Court. She joined the Boalt faculty in 1960 and received the UC Berkeley Distinguished Teaching Award in 1962. She served as dean of Boalt Hall from 1992 to 2000. In 2003 the Boalt Hall Alumni Association presented her with its first Faculty Lifetime Achievement Award. In 1998 Professor Kay was named one of the 50 most influential female lawyers in the country and one of the eight most influential lawyers in Northern California by the National Law Journal. She served as president of the Association of American Law Schools in 1989 and as secretary of the American Bar Association (ABA) Section on Legal Education and Admissions to the Bar from 1999 to 2001. Professor Kay is currently a member of the Council of the American Law Institute. She has received many major awards, including the Society of American Law Teachers Teaching Award, the 1990 American Bar Foundation Research Award, and the 1992 Margaret Brent Award to Women Lawyers of Distinction

from the ABA Commission on Women in the Profession. In 2000 she was elected to membership in the American Philosophical Society. Professor Kay has been a fellow at the Center for Advanced Study in Behavioral Sciences and a visiting professor at Harvard University, Lewis & Clark University, and Hamline University. She served on the faculty of the Salzburg Seminar on American Law in 1987. She is a past or present member of 12 different governing or advisory boards, including the Russell Sage Foundation, Equal Rights Advocates, Inc., Order of the Coif, and the American Academy of Arts and Sciences. In 2003 the Boalt Hall Alumni Association presented her with its first Faculty Lifetime Achievement Award at the annual Citation Award Dinner. In 2005, she received the Rutter Award for Teaching Distinction at Boalt Hall, and in 2007, the Berkeley Academic Senate presented its Faculty Service award to her. Professor Kay received a J.D. from the University of Chicago, where she ranked third in her class and was Book Review editor of the Chicago Law Review.

CELEBRATING EARLY WOMEN LAW STUDENTS AND LAW PROFESSORS

I am so honored to be here for this Kate Stoneman Award Day and I am particularly delighted to join you in celebrating the dedication of the 10th anniversary of the award to Chief Judge Judith Kaye of the New York Court of Appeals. Chief Judge Kaye and I served together on the Council of the American Law Institute when we were working on the Principles of Family Dissolution.[1] It was a great disappointment to me that she felt she had to resign from the council because she had taken on this other job—being chief judge of New York—that she thought might interfere with her time. I never had the slightest doubt that she was capable of doing both. We certainly missed her. I even think there were a few things that got through the council that might not have gotten through had Chief Judge Kaye's keen eye read it.

I see that today's audience is primarily female, and I want to say just a word, by way of commiseration, to those of you in the audience who belong to what we sometimes call the "opposite sex." I'm reminded of this wonderful story told by Professor Alison Grey Anderson of UCLA:[2]

Several years ago at UCLA a young male student had a complaint about a class (I don't remember the nature of the complaint, but I don't think it was gender-related.). He spoke first with Assistant Dean of Students Barbara Koshela, was unsatisfied, and went next to see Associate Dean Carole Goldberg-Ambrose and ultimately Dean Susan Prager. Apparently his problem was not resolved to his satisfaction, and after seeing Dean Prager, he emerged from her office, looked around and exclaimed plaintively, "Isn't there a man around here I can talk to?"

So maybe with all these wonderful accomplishments by women we're celebrating here today, we have to remember to be sensitive to the needs of our male law colleagues and students and see to it that they don't feel too isolated and silenced by the rest of us.

In preparing for today's keynote address, I read Chief Judge Kaye's excellent 1994 Stoneman Lecture.[3] What I learned there about Kate Stoneman and her exceptional pioneering career makes me very proud to accept this award given in her name. Her story is especially meaningful to those of us from California because there are some quite remarkable similarities between her path to becoming New York's first woman lawyer in 1886 and the route followed by Clara Shortridge Foltz in becoming California's first woman lawyer in 1878.[4]

Both women were confronted by statutes expressly limiting admission to the bar to men. You would think that this barrier might have discouraged most women from trying to be lawyers, and no doubt it did. Neither of these two women, however, was deterred in the slightest by this obstacle. Instead, both drafted and successfully lobbied for the enactment of bills opening membership in the bar to women. Kate Stoneman's bill was broader, as it also abolished barriers to the legal profession based on race. Both then applied as students to law school after becoming lawyers, not uncommon in those days. In this effort, Foltz encountered an additional obstacle. She wanted to go to the Hastings College of the Law, which prohibited admission to women, so she had to sue Hastings to get in. She won her case, arguing it before the California Supreme Court in 1879.[5] Unlike Stoneman, however, Foltz never entered law school. By that time she had her eye on another prize, helping to draft the California State Constitution of 1879.

She went to work as a clerk with the Judiciary Committee and was responsible for what is now Article 22, Section 18 of the California Constitution, which provides that, "No person shall, on account of sex, be disqualified from entering upon or pursuing any lawful business, vocation or profession." Stoneman went on to graduate, of course, from Albany Law School in 1898 and embarked upon a second career as an eloquent advocate for women's rights.

I will take my topic today from the inspiring example of these two early women lawyers. In doing so, I am mindful of Chief Judge Kaye's concluding footnote in her keynote address in which she observed "It continues to disappoint me that no law school (to my knowledge) has, as yet, undertaken to establish a definitive collection on women in the law."[6] I can't claim that we've done that at Berkeley, either, Judge Kaye, but at least I'm working on part of it. I would now like to share with you some of my research on early women law professors.

Early Women Law Professors

Fifteen years ago, in 1989, I served a term as president of the Association of American Law Schools. In giving press interviews about that event, I was frequently asked whether I was the first woman to hold that office. The question was not unreasonable. At that point, few women had held positions of leadership in legal education. But the correct answer was "No." In fact, I was the third woman to serve as president of the AALS. Soia Mentschikoff was the first. She preceded me by fifteen years, becoming president in 1974 when she was dean of the University of Miami Law School. The second woman president was that very same earlier-mentioned Professor Susan Westerberg Prager of UCLA, who later became their dean. She followed Soia twelve years later, holding the office in 1986. I served as a member of Susan's Executive Committee and learned a great deal from her excellent example about how to do the job.

Looking back, I think it was actually while I was patiently recounting the brief history of woman AALS presidents to reporters that I first began to wonder who the other early woman law professors had been. In my own mind, I thought of them as the women who had started teaching before I did, that is, before 1960. I began making a list of them. I had no problem identifying the first one, because she had been my colleague at Berkeley. Barbara Nachtrieb Armstrong began her teaching career as a joint lecturer in the Department of Economics and the School of Jurisprudence in 1919. She had retired from teaching by the time I joined the faculty, but she had kept her faculty office and was busily engaged in updating her two-volume work on California family law. Who, I wondered, were the women who began teaching law between Barbara and me?

I went first to the *AALS Directory of Law Teachers*, which began publication of its list of all teachers in member schools in 1922. I quickly learned that the first women to work at professional staff positions at law schools were law librarians. That actually was the case here at Albany, where a woman law librarian preceded the first woman law professor. Catherine Nugent Haiss was appointed as instructor in law and law librarian in 1958. Albany's second woman law librarian, Anita L. Morse, was appointed as assistant professor and law librarian in 1974, the same year that Sandy Stevenson became the first woman faculty member. Since the training and career paths of law librarians are different from those of regular faculty, I refined my definition to include only women who were full-time, tenure or tenure-track professors at law schools that were approved by the ABA and members of the AALS (ABA/AALS schools). After supplementing the data I found in the directory with questions to colleagues around the country, I have identified fourteen women, including Barbara, who fit that definition. These fourteen are the women that I have called "early women law professors."[7] Today, when I show this list to other law professors, both women and men of varying ages and locations, I find that very few people recognize all fourteen names. So, just for fun, I thought I'd try an experiment this afternoon. I'll read you the names of these fourteen women, together with the year of their initial appointment at an ABA/AALS school, and ask you to raise your hand if you have ever heard of this particular woman:

1. Barbara Nachtrieb Armstrong, Berkeley, 1919.
2. Harriet Spiller Daggett, Louisiana State University, 1926.
3. Margaret Harris Amsler, Baylor, 1941.
4. Soia Mentschikoff, Harvard, 1947, Chicago, 1951.
5. Jeanette Ozanne Smith, University of Miami, 1949.
6. Clemence Myers Smith, Loyola, Los Angeles, 1952.
7. Ellen Ash Peters, Yale, 1956.

8. Janet Mary Riley, Loyola, New Orleans, 1956.
9. Helen Elsie Steinbinder, Georgetown, 1956.
10. Dorothy Wright Nelson, University of Southern California, 1957.
11. Joan M. Krauskopf, Ohio State University, 1958.
12. Maria Minnette Massey, University of Miami, 1958.
13. Marygold Melli, Wisconsin, 1959.
14. Miriam Theresa Rooney, Seton Hall, 1959.

Well, you see, your response proves my point. This is a story that's rapidly disappearing, which is why I need to get on with writing my book. Like you, almost everybody recognizes the name of Soia Mentschikoff. As my colleague, Frank Zimring[8] once said of her when he was on the Chicago faculty, "She's the first woman everything." Most of the other women on my list are remembered primarily by people at the schools where they taught. Two of them, Ellen Peters and Dorothy Nelson, left law teaching to become judges, and they are known today more widely from their time on the bench than from their earlier academic careers.

Today I want to give you just a bit of the flavor of that work by sharing a few stories (which will appear in the book) from the lives and careers of some of these women. I'll start with Barbara Armstrong. Barbara had been on the Berkeley faculty from 1919 until she retired in 1957. She was at Berkeley, working on the second edition of her family law treatise, when I was hired there in 1960. Barbara had made it very clear to her colleagues that she intended to be followed by a woman who would take over her courses in Family Law and California Marital Property. As I have recounted elsewhere,[9] Professor Richard W. Jennings, who chaired the Berkeley Faculty Appointments Committee at the time, said that while the committee "didn't have any agenda about women," he supposed that "there was an agenda so far as when Barbara retired." In 1959, the Appointments Committee located me while clerking for their former colleague (and Barbara's close friend) Justice Roger J. Traynor of the California Supreme Court. Upon his recommendation, I was invited to interview for a teaching position.

So, I went over to Berkeley for my day of interviews. In those days we didn't have faculty job talks. Candidates went around from office to office, and went out to lunch with the faculty, and if you flunked lunch, that was the end of you, right? Well, I didn't flunk lunch, but if it hadn't been for Barbara's swift intervention, I might have flunked the dress code. Remember, I was clerking for the prestigious California Supreme Court, located in the stylish city of San Francisco, and I was in the habit of wearing hats to work. And I had, by actual count, 28 hats. Since I wanted to make a good impression, I had chosen one of my special favorites to wear to the interviews. It was a sort of wide top crushed velvet hat with a beautiful brim that came down nearly to my eyebrows: really, an elegant hat. At about 4 in the afternoon, just before I was to attend the faculty reception, I was in Barbara's office having tea. She confronted me with some timely advice. She said, "You have to take your hat off. The men want to see what you look like." It was a very warm day in Berkeley and I knew my hair would be damply plastered to my head if I removed my hat, and I would look just terrible. I apologized. "Well, Professor Armstrong, I can't take my hat off. My hair would just, you know, I just can't do it." Barbara gave me an appraising look and then she said, "Very well. Perhaps when you come back for your second day of interviews you could wear a smaller hat." "Oh, of course, Professor Armstrong," I said, "but I didn't know there was going to be a second day of interviews." "There will be, now," Barbara said firmly. So, there was a second day of interviews, I wore a small hat, I was hired, and without Barbara it wouldn't have happened.

Now, here's the Soia Mentshikoff story, which is also about mentoring. I heard it in 1989 from Lillian Kraemer, who graduated from the University of Chicago Law School in 1964, was first in her class and a member of the *Chicago Law Review,* and who became a very successful partner in New York City.[10] But despite her outstanding credentials, when she was a second year student looking for a summer job with a Wall Street law firm, she had no success. One afternoon, she came back to the law school after a particularly frustrating day of job seeking and she was furious. She was carrying a stack of books as she entered the law review office, and she stormed into the office, throwing books everywhere. She was berating her colleagues: "You guys are all getting jobs. I'm never going to get any jobs. I rank higher in the class than you do. What am I going to do?" And somebody (who had ducked behind a desk) said, "Calm down! Why don't you go and ask Professor Mentschikoff?" So Lillian marched up to Soia's office, introduced herself as a second year student, and asked "What in the world do I have to do to get a job on Wall Street?" Soia asked, "Where do you stand in the class?" Lillian replied, "I'm first." Thereupon, Soia gave her this advice: "Wear a little black dress that subtly does something for you and a small silver pin." Lillian was astonished. This was not the advice she had expected. "What do you mean?" she asked. "What does this have to do with my ability to be a lawyer? What do I say? How do I convince them I'm serious?" And Soia replied, patiently, "Lillian, have you tried wearing a little black dress and a small silver pin?" "No." "Well, try it and come back and tell me what happens." The very next week, Lillian got herself a black dress and a small silver pin. She immediately received several job offers. And she was even more confused. She went back to Soia and asked, "Miss Mentschikoff, how do you explain this?" Soia smiled. "From that day to this," Lillian Kraemer added, "I have never interviewed in anything other than a black dress and a small silver pin, and I have never not gotten an offer since that time."

My final story is about Margo Melli from Wisconsin. Margo actually was not on my initial list of 14 women. The first article I published about my research listed only 13 women before 1960.[11] And then Margo decided to retire and some of her colleagues called me to ask if I had anything about Margo that they could use at her retirement dinner. And I said, "Margo's not on my list. She didn't start teaching at Wisconsin until 1961." "Oh, no," they said, "she started here in 1959." Well, the *AALS Directory* said 1961. So I called up Margo (of course I knew her since we were both in family law) and I said "Margo, what's going on here?" "Well, Herma," she said, "it's true. I did start teaching in Wisconsin in 1959 as a tenure-track assistant professor, but then Joe (Joe was her classmate whom she had married) and I decided to adopt a child and the adoption agency would not place an infant with a dual-career couple. So (she said), I resigned my appointment, took a leave of absence, got the baby, was reappointed in 1961, and the school never corrected the date." Isn't that remarkable? There has to be a special chapter, I think, about this. After I called this error to the attention of some folks at Wisconsin, they managed to correct the record, so if you look at the current *AALS Directory*, it now states that she was appointed in 1959.

The First Women at Each School

My story about women law professors doesn't stop with 1959. I plan to cover the period 1900 through 2000. I'm necessarily treating the women who began teaching in the last part of the twentieth century— those who began between 1960 and 2000—more statistically. One of the individual things I am doing, however, is identifying the "first woman" professor at each of the AALS/ABA law schools. As I'm sure all of you are aware, the first woman to be appointed to a tenure-track position here at Albany was Professor Sandra Stevenson. Like most of the fourteen early women law professors, Sandy was a graduate of the school that hired her as its first woman professor. She graduated from Albany in 1971 and took up her appointment here as an assistant professor in 1974. She was among the first group of women to be hired in significant numbers by law schools around the country. Double digit hiring of women faculty first occurred in 1970, when fifteen women began teaching in ABA/AALS schools across the country. Two independent events contributed to this increase in the rate of hiring of women. In December, 1970, the AALS prohibited its member schools from discriminating on the basis of sex in admissions, employment, and placement. And, in 1972, Congress amended Title VII of the Civil Rights Act to apply to institutions of higher education. By 1974, the year that Sandy was hired here, the total number of women listed as new hires in the AALS directory came to 55, a figure that exceeds by four the total number of women hired during the 50-year period between 1919 and 1969. Clearly, something new was happening in the rarified atmosphere of legal education. Although their cumulative numbers were large, however, many of these fledgling women law professors were being hired one at a time by their schools. In some of the earlier work that I've published on this project, I've measured the time gap between a law school's founding date and the date on which it hired its first and then its second woman faculty member.[12] Albany Law School was founded in 1851 and Professor Stevenson was hired in 1974, a time gap of 123 years. Now, while you may think that this is a relatively long time gap, it's not the longest. Harvard has the record. Its faculty remained all male for over a century and a half. But if Albany's initial time gap was lengthy, to its credit, it moved swiftly to add a second woman to the faculty. In 1975, Professor Katheryn D. Katz was appointed as assistant professor. She had graduated from Albany in 1970.

Sandy and Kathy met each other as students here at Albany Law School, where Kathy was a year ahead of Sandy. Both were on the *Albany Law Review*, Sandy as an associate editor and Kathy as comments editor. Kathy earned her B.A. from my school—Cal. Berkeley—in 1955, and began her law school education as a young mother at the University of New Mexico Law School in the late 1960s. She was the only woman in her class and felt that she was "completely ignored" by her teachers and classmates. She transferred to Albany as a second year student where the atmosphere was completely different. Although there were no women on the faculty, there were seven or eight women students in her class and she and Sandy became close friends. After graduation she and another Albany graduate, Margrethe R. Powers, class of '63, became the first women to found a law firm in upstate New York.

After her graduation in 1971, Sandy accepted a position as assistant special counsel to the New York State Department of Environmental Conservation and helped draft New York's first environmental conservation law. After the project was completed, she accepted a faculty position at Rensselaer Polytechnic Institute (R.P.I.) in 1973 as assistant professor of management. And it's possible, although Sandy isn't sure of this, that she may have been the first woman full-time professor at R.P.I., as well as the first woman law professor at Albany. While at R.P.I., she taught graduate courses in environmental law and business law and was responsible for helping to launch the R.P.I./Albany Law School accelerated degree program, which allows a student applying for admission to both programs to receive his/her undergraduate law degrees in six years. That program is still in existence. When Sandy accepted Albany's offer to teach here, she invited Kathy to lunch. And here's a story of powerful female networking. She suggested that Kathy might be interested in applying for her soon-to-be vacated position at R.P.I. Kathy was, and did. She found that she loved teaching. She recalled that she had never considered a teaching career, because she had never had a single woman professor in law school. The possibility didn't occur to her. I, of course, had Soia Mentschikoff at Chicago as a role model. When Albany invited her to join the faculty in 1975, Kathy jumped at the opportunity and she and Sandy have been faculty colleagues here for nearly 30 years. The 2003-2004 *AALS Directory* lists 21 women who are members of the Albany law faculty. Twelve of them hold clinical or lawyering titles, and nine are tenure or tenure-track faculty members. Of these nine, only four—Sandy, Kathy, Patricia Salkin and Beverly Cohen—are graduates of Albany.

In the years when women were rarely seen on law faculties, many law schools turned to the women they had trained—and therefore knew well intellectually—to form their faculty pool. Here Albany graduates are a minority among the women faculty. Like most of the 14 early women law professors, Sandy has devoted a great deal of time and effort to law reform. She was the founding director of the Government Law Center and served as director and associate dean from 1985 through 1990. She also developed the internationally recognized Saratoga Conferences and initiated a science technology and law focus at the law school. When I finally complete my work on early women law professors, I will proudly add Sandy and Kathy to my story of early women at each individual law school with their tale of how two women working together are more powerful than one woman working alone.

Notes

1. AM. L. INST., PRINCIPLES OF THE LAW OF FAMILY DISSOLUTION: ANALYSIS AND RECOMMENDATIONS (2002).

2. *Quoted in* Herma Hill Kay, *UC's Women Law Professors*, 36 U.C. DAVIS L. REV. 331, 397 (2003).

3. *See* Judith Kaye, *How to Accomplish Success: The Example of Kate Stoneman*, 57 ALBANY L. REV. 961 (1994).

4. *See* Barbara Allen Babcock, *Clara Shortridge Foltz: "First Woman,"* 30 ARIZ. L. REV. 673 (1988).

5. *Id.* at 705-15; *see also* THOMAS G. BARNES, HASTINGS COLLEGE OF THE LAW: THE FIRST CENTURY (1978).

6. *See* Kaye, *supra* note 3, at 971 & n. 45.

7. *See* Kay, *supra* note 2, at 337.

8. *See* Connie Bruck, *Soia Mentschikoff: The First Woman Everything*, AM. LAW. 32, 33 (1982) (quoting Frank Zimring).

9. *See* Kay, *supra* note 2, at 341.

10. Interview with Lillian Kraemer, New York City, Dec. 4, 1989. *See also* Bruck, *supra* note 8 (recounting a similar version of this story told to her by Lillian Kraemer).

11. *See* Herma Hill Kay, *The Future of Women Law Professors*, 77 IOWA L. REV. 5, 8 (1991).

12. *See* Kay, *supra* note 2, at 339-42; Herma Hill Kay, *Ruth Bader Ginsburg, Professor of Law*, 104 COLUM. L. REV. 2, 5 (Table 1) (2004).

Professor Margaret E. Montoya 2006 **12**

Margaret E. Montoya is a professor of law at the University of New Mexico (UNM) School of Law with a second-

ary appointment in the Department of Family and Community Medicine in the School of Medicine. A member of the UNM law school faculty since 1992, Professor Montoya examines issues of race, ethnicity, gender, and language, along with cross-cultural discourse in her scholarship and teaching. She often teaches seminars on these subjects. During college at San Diego State University in the 1970s, she was a member of the student government and was involved in the Chicano, anti-war, and women's movements. Since institutions are integrated by groups and not lone pioneers, she joined other "firsts" when she became the first Hispanic woman accepted at Harvard Law School. After graduation, she received the Harvard University Frederick Sheldon Traveling Fellowship and studied affirmative action in India and Malaysia. In Mexico, Boston, and Potsdam, New York, she worked in corporate law, legal services, and academic administration before returning home to New Mexico. She was the UNM associate university counsel for employment issues before joining the law faculty. She has con-

tributed to a number of anthologies and casebooks on legal topics involving race and gender and brings a continuing interest in these areas to her teaching. Her particular areas of expertise are affirmative action and the emerging area of critical race pedagogy. Professor Montoya served as the 2003-2004 interim director of the Southwest Hispanic Research Institute. The institute was established in 1980 to serve as the interdisciplinary center for the study of the Hispanic experience in the Southwest. The broad purpose of the institute is to promote teaching and research and to disseminate information that impacts Hispanic peoples and communities in the southwestern states of Texas, New Mexico, Colorado, Arizona, and California and in Latin America, especially Mexico. While director, she helped develop a "pipeline" program linking the law school with the medical school in reaching out to form partnerships with the public schools. She appears in a weekly PBS television news program called "NM in Focus." Professor Montoya received an A.B. in 1972 from San Diego State University and a J.D. in 1978 from Harvard Law School. She is a member of the bars of Massachusetts, New York, and New Mexico.

WHY KATE STONEMAN WOULD HAVE LIKED THE MOVIE "NORTH COUNTRY"

Buenas tardes y mil gracias por invitarme a participar en este programa para celebrar las mujeres y nuestros valores feministas. I am delighted to be here. I thank my friends and the selection committee at Albany Law School for extending this honor to me and the other accomplished recipients.

Thank you to Judge Kaye and the other appellate court judges and lawyers of the New York bar, the dean, faculty, staff, and students of the Albany Law School and the women and men of the Albany community for taking this opportunity to honor the vision and activism of Kate Stoneman. This annual celebration provides us with an opportunity to reflect on issues of equity and how the law can be a force for both justice and injustice.

Kate Stoneman was 44 years old when, in 1885, she took and passed the New York state bar examination. By that time, she was an experienced community activist, leader of the Albany suffragists, and a teacher in Albany's Normal School, preparing teachers for the public schools. Her teaching career would last some 40 years and help support her while she worked to become an attorney. By 1885, Kate Stoneman had five years of experience drafting suffrage bills and lobbying for their passage. She was well known by the legislators and, therefore, well positioned to challenge the decision of the New York Supreme Court, which denied her application to become a member of the bar. To become a lawyer, Kate Stoneman would first have to amend the state Code of Civil Procedure, which had been revised in 1871 to explicitly limit the office of attorney to "any male citizen."

Anticipating this outcome, the women had drawn up a bill and found John Platt, a friendly assemblyman, to introduce it. The bill remained in the judiciary committee for six months and, on the day after Stoneman's rejection, Platt moved for its final reading and it passed with a vote of 78 to 6. Six days later, on May 18 (as the legislature was about to adjourn), the senate passed the bill with no dissenting votes. Getting the governor to sign the bill required the political savvy of a community organizer, and Stoneman was up to the challenge. She and her suffragist friends rounded up the mayor, Assemblyman Platt, other legislators, and members of the press and called on the governor. Hearing from Stoneman that her wish was "chiefly to extend the field of women's activity. . ." satisfied the governor and he signed the bill. Kate Stoneman thanked him "in the name of the women of N.Y. State."

Nine days after she had been denied admission, Kate Stoneman and her friends had amended the relevant statute, she reapplied for admission, and on May 20 was admitted to the bar by order of the Supreme Court.

Kate Stoneman's story illustrates vividly that the law in its different forms has been a barrier for women trying to gain employment in male-dominated professions. Kate Stoneman's story is the story of workplace equity—changing the law has often been a precondition to opening the workplace to women. This was true for Kate Stoneman, and it was also true for Lois Jenson, one of the first women hired in the Eveleth iron mines in northern Minnesota. A series of lawsuits were settled in 1974 and the ensuing consent decree required the steel companies and unions to hire women and minorities.

Lois Jenson and the other women hired under these affirmative action goals worked in an environment of intolerable sexual abuse and incessant harassment. After enduring nine years of brutalizing abuse and dreading that she would lose her job, she began doing research in the library, and, in 1984, filed a complaint with the Minnesota Human Rights Department. After investigating, the department ordered Eveleth to pay $11,000. The company refused.

It took Kate Stoneman nine days to win her dispute, but it would take Lois Jenson 14 years; it would cost her mental and physical health, she would have to contact 50 lawyers before finding Paul Sprenger, and then he would have to make new law by filing the first sexual harassment lawsuit to be certified as a class action before Lois Jenson would finally find some justice.

In 1992 the trial judge ruled against the employer on liability and in 1993 a special master began the damages phase of the case. Eveleth's lead counsel was a woman who was determined to prove that the women miners' behavior caused the harassment and that they were lying about the severity of its effects. She was aided by the special master who permitted her to probe the medical histories, the personal lives, and sexual experiences of the plaintiffs. Then, after describing the plaintiffs as "histrionic," he awarded the plaintiffs an average of only $10,000. In 1997, the Eighth Circuit, finding numerous errors by the special master, rejected the damages and ordered a trial de novo before a jury. The following year Eveleth settled with the plaintiffs for $3.5 million. It is estimated that the three trials cost Eveleth more than $15 million in legal fees and settlement costs.

Lois Jenson's struggles became the basis for a book, *Class Action*," and most recently inspired the movie, *North Country,* with Charlize Theron as the lead character.

BHP Billiton is an extractive resources company with reported profits of $11 billion in 2005; BHP mines coal in Africa, Australia, Colombia, and the Navajo Nation. In 1963, surface mining began at Navajo Mine to supply the Four Corners Power Plant. Today the mines, located on or near the Navajo Indian Reservation in the northwest corner of New Mexico, are owned and run by BHP Billiton. According to the company's web page, some 65 per cent of the workforce is Native American; other reports make estimates as high as 90 percent.

On January 31, 2004, the workers in Local 983 went on strike for the first time. They rejected the contract offered by BHP because of inadequate wages, an underfunded pension plan, and diluted health benefits, especially in the coverage of traditional indigenous healing. After 12 days, the union ended its strike, agreeing to a wage increase, better health coverage, and protection of Navajo hiring preferences.

The Militant, a socialist newspaper, in reporting about the strike wrote, "Despite the abundance of natural resources on their lands, many Navajos live in conditions that in some respects resemble those in underdeveloped countries. According to the 2000-2001 Comprehensive Economic Development Strategy Report from the Navajo Nation Division of Economic Development, 56 percent of Navajos live below the poverty level, per capita income is $6,217, and unemployment is 43 percent. These figures underscore the importance of preferential hiring."

The Navajo nation has the biggest reserves of coal of any tribe. During the 1990s leases and royalties, set at 12.5 percent, netted the tribe about $80 million per year; coal mining is its biggest income-producer. Some 5,000 Navajos work for energy companies on the reservation. Because of the widespread unemployment, poverty, and lack of such basic infrastructure as electricity or running water, the relatively high wage jobs offered by the coal mines have proven indispensable to Navajo families. By the early 1970s, the jobs attracted Navajo women workers.

Rosie Kellywood Foster is a heavy-equipment operator who has worked at the BHP San Juan surface mine for 14 years. She runs track dozers, motor graders, and 170-ton haul trucks. She says it took a fight on her part to get a coal mining job. "It has been hard for women here to get hired in the mines," she has told us. "The companies think that this not the kind of work women can do. And there are some Navajo male co-workers who also believe women shouldn't work here. I always thought of myself as a victim, but I got tired of this."

Last year after learning that I might be someone who could speak about sexual harassment, Rosie called me and told me the Navajo women coal miners were trying to organize an employment law conference. Coincidentally, I was teaching a class on employment discrimination. I mentioned that, instead of taking final exams, I require the students to collaborate on service learning projects and that I would ask the students to call her. Once they talked with Rosie, the students agreed to help with the conference. Eventually, the students helped identify speakers, raised money, wrote the agenda and program materials, and participated in and videotaped the day-long conference in Farmington, New Mexico.

The conference theme was "Changing Woman," the central figure in one of the Navajo origin stories. In the Navajo tradition, Changing Woman represents the beginning of life from nothingness. While mysterious and enigmatic, she is woman, the embodiment of hope.

The conference began with a convocation by a Navajo elder followed by the pledge of allegiance in Navajo by the student of the year. The presentations included a lecture on cultural and indigenous knowledge, followed by sessions on mental health by a Navajo medical doctor and psychologist, another by EEOC representatives on formal remedies to discrimination, and one in which I explained sexual harassment law and offered practical responses to workplace harassment (such as the three-part letter in which a victim of harassment describes the specific incident in detail, tells the harasser how it made her feel, and then tells him that if he doesn't refrain from such behavior, she will take certain action such as talking with supervisors, filing a grievance, etc.)

During the lunch break, in keeping with the Navajo trait of finding laughter and joy in any situation, we were offered entertainment. Rosie's husband began with a stand-up comedy routine and ended with an Elvis impersonation. Dressed in a white cape and wide belt that has come to be classic Elvis, he proceeded to sing "Love Me Tender" and "Hound Dog"—in Navajo. It was terrific and the audience loved it.

Today the Navajo women coal miners are being represented by the EEOC, which is investigating their claims of employment discrimination and sexual harassment. In order not to jeopardize their claims, I can't say much about the work conditions in the coal mines.

On April 24, 2006, we will convene at the San Juan Community College for the second annual "Changing Woman" conference. One group of students in my gender and the law seminar is again helping with the arrangements. This year one keynoter is Lois Jenson, who will bring her story about the mines of the north country of Minnesota to share with the Navajo women.

Through the international advocacy undertaken by my colleague Professor Christine Zuni Cruz (Isleta, Okay Owingeh) and her husband Robert Cruz (Tohono O'odham), we were connected with a second keynoter, Rosalina Tuyuc from Guatemala. She will link the Navajo women's struggle in the north country of New Mexico with the struggle of indigenous women throughout the hemisphere. Rosalina Tuyuc, a Maya-Kaqchikel, has fought for 20 years to have the state admit its responsibility for the detention, disappearance, and death of thousands of Guatemaltecos. She has concentrated her efforts on fighting to gain respect for women and the well-being of the indigenous peoples. Before serving as an elected deputy in the congress, Tuyuc founded Conavigua—the National Coalition of Guatemalan Widows. She describes her struggle as a "fight against the indifference to the weakest in the society— the children of widows who often can't express their pain or suffering." She says her place is "at the side of widows and women who carry the weight of racism on their shoulders." Rosalina identifies with and advocates for the women and children missing their male relatives because she, too, is a child who continues to miss her father and is still looking for him among 300 clandestine cemeteries, which resulted from U.S. intervention in Guatemala (indigenous peoples in the U.S. have also had to deal with illegitimate state power).

In my teaching, one of my chief objectives is to teach the students to use critical race theory and Latino/Latina critical legal theory (what we call "LatCrit") to understand "garden variety" legal problems. Critical race theory can often seem esoteric and remote; theory is dense with jargon and a specialized vocabulary. I bring this scholarship into the classroom so that students can link issues of identity, culture, and racial power to the subjects they are studying and the communities they are serving. It is not enough that they understand Title VII doctrine and EEOC procedures; they must understand how race, gender, class, and sexuality frame the struggles of real people—women such as Kate Stoneman, Lois Jenson, Rosie Kellywood Foster, and Rosalina Tuyuc. All of them had to work to fund their activism.

Our gender and the law class begins with theory—the students are trained through two different discourses: a case book with a traditional feminist analysis and a reader on critical race feminism. They are expected to bring issues of identity, culture and racial power to bear on the discussion of such topics as women and their bodies, women and the family, and women and work.

Many students enter the class feeling unable to make cogent arguments about such hot button issues as abortion, affirmative action, and workplace equity. So we work in and out of class to understand how to use legal arguments, data and statistics, and stories to inform and persuade. And we sometimes conclude that some arguments are not winnable and the best thing to do is walk away. We look for situations that allow students to connect abstract and theoretical analyses with issues they are facing in their everyday lives, such as whether and how they as women of color belong in law school and the legal profession. Because these issues trigger strong emotions, learning to be an effective communicator requires practice. Legal questions that implicate one's identity, family, tribal, or community history and intergenerational trauma require greater analytical sophistication than briefing cases and extracting legal rules. Students must learn to synthesize different types of information—cases, theory, narratives, their own feelings and intuition, and the knowledge they bring from their home communities. They have to learn to become comfortable hearing their voices in public spaces. The students of color must learn to function and speak on behalf of others (and often themselves) in spaces that are unfamiliar and forbidding. Students of color must also learn the skills to work with communities of color different than their own; they must learn to be both insiders and outsiders; they must recognize and correct color-on-color racism.

The students experience the power of law and they hone the range of skills and competencies they already possess by combining them with the doctrines, theories, and skills they are learning in law school as they address the needs of under-served communities. Thus, one group is working on the Navajo women coal miner's conference, another is working with Latino and Native families to create a *Parents' Handbook on Higher Education*, and a third group is working with a school-based health clinic to create a students' guide to legal rights and responsibilities.

I began this talk by saying that the law is a force for both justice and injustice. This is a foundational proposition in critical race theory and LatCrit. Each of the four women I have mentioned—Kate Stoneman, Lois Jenson, Rosie Kellywood Foster, and Rosalina Tuyuc—have been subjected to prolonged injustices. Each of the four undertook to use the law to expand opportunities for women. Kate Stoneman and Lois Jenson both used lawsuits to reform the law and transformed the workplace. Rosie Foster is using community legal education to improve the chances that the Native women will persist and prevail in their complaints about employment discrimination. Rosalina Tuyuc became a legislator in the national congress of Guatemala to win rights for widows and other indigenous women.

When Kate Stoneman sought to "extend the field of women's activity" she was linked by her courage and boldness to the generations of women who have struggled in such different workplaces as the iron mines of Minnesota, the coal mines of the Navajo nation and the pueblitos of Guatemala. Today, we honor Kate Stoneman by finding her face among the faces of women around the world who have broken the silence about the injustices endured by women, widows and their children. We honor Kate Stoneman by re-telling her story to find inspiration for the contemporary struggles that face women. We honor Kate Stoneman by gathering in her memory, celebrating the advances women have made, and resolving to continue the work of expanding justice and equity.

Mil gracias. Thank you very much.

Appendix

The following 48 women and men have been recognized by Albany Law School from 1994 to 2007 for their outstanding contributions to ensuring equity and fairness in the legal profession for women of all races, ages and religions. All of the people recognized have been role models and mentors for women attorneys and aspiring attorneys, and have served as an inspiration to others. They have all exemplified the wonderful qualities of Kate Stoneman and serve as a reminder that people can make a difference and that there is much more to be done.

Kate Stoneman Award Honorees

1994
Bernard E. Harvith*
Hon. Judith S. Kaye
Helen M. Pratt '28*

1995
Katheryn D. Katz '70
Hon. Jeanine F. Pirro '75

1996
Donna J. Morse*
Miriam M. Netter '72
M. Catherine Richardson

1997
Gloria Herron Arthur '85
Charlotte S. Buchanan '80
Hon. Constance Baker Motley*

1998
Kate Stoneman
Graduation Centennial
Judy Clarke
Rachel Kretser
Karen J. Mathis
Lillian M. Moy
Margrethe Powers '63*
Marjorie Semerad*
Sandra M. Stevenson '71
Hon. Beverly C. Tobin '62

1999
Martha W. Barnett
Hon. Victoria A. Graffeo '77
Kathryn Grant Madigan '78
Mary Helen Moses

2000
Martha F. Davis
Hon. Mary O. Donohue '83

* Deceased

2002

Penelope Andrews
Gail Brown Bensen
Georgia Nucci '96
Patricia Youngblood Reyhan
Hon. Mary Jo White

2003

Hon. Carmen Ciparick
Carol E. Dinkins
Hon. Yvonne Mokgoro
Lorraine Power Tharp
Winifred R. Widmer '54

Fall 2004

Herma Hill Kay
Nancy K. Ota
Dianne Otto
Dianne R. Phillips '88
Donna E. Wardlaw '77

Spring 2006

Margaret Montoya
Betty Lugo '84
Hon. Karen K. Peters
Ann Shalleck

Spring 2007

Marina Angel
Cheryl D. Mills
Hon. Leslie E. Stein '81
Sharon P. Stiller '75